Crocheting Bedspreads

Edited by
Rita Weiss

Dover Publications, Inc.
New York

American terminology, which is different from crochet terminology in most other parts of the world, is used for the stitches in this book. The following chart supplies the American name of crochet stitches and their equivalent in other countries. Crocheters should become thoroughly familiar with the differences in these terms before starting on any project.

AMERICAN NAME	EQUIVALENT
Chain	same
Slip	Single crochet
Single crochet	Double crochet
Half-double or short-double crochet	Half-treble crochet
Double crochet	Treble crochet
Treble crochet	Double-treble crochet
Double-treble crochet	Treble-treble crochet
Treble-treble or long-treble crochet	Quadruple-treble crochet
Afghan stitch	Tricot crochet

Published in Canada by General Publishing Company, Ltd., 30 Lesmill Road, Don Mills, Toronto, Ontario.
Published in the United Kingdom by Constable and Company, Ltd., 10 Orange Street, London WC2H 7EG.

This Dover edition, first published in 1978, is a new selection of patterns from *Bedspreads to Knit and Crochet*, published by the Spool Cotton Company in 1941; *Bedspreads*, published by the Spool Cotton Company in 1939 and *Bedspreads to Knit and Crochet*, published by the Spool Cotton Company in 1939. This edition also contains a new introduction.

International Standard Book Number: 0-486-23610-2
Library of Congress Catalog Card Number: 77-88742

Manufactured in the United States of America
Dover Publications, Inc.
180 Varick Street
New York, N.Y. 10014

Introduction

This is a new collection of some of the loveliest crocheted bedspread patterns published in instruction brochures over thirty years ago, during the period when the making of hand crocheted bedspreads was an extremely popular pastime. The crocheted bedspread, done in the grand manner, has remained the classic covering for a fine bed, and today as we return once again to the joys of creating exquisite handmade articles, the crocheting of bedspreads is enjoying a new surge of popularity.

A crocheted bedspread is a real investment in beauty because it wears practically forever, remaining a classic while other bedspread fashions come and go. A crocheted bedspread need not be treated with "touch-me-not" reverence! It will outwear practically any other kind of spread and wash like a charm. Best of all, a crocheted bedspread has that elusive, intrinsic quality that comes with handmade things.

Although most of the threads listed with the patterns are still available, you may wish to substitute some of the newer cottons, synthetics and polyesters now on the market. Check with your local needlework shop or department. Whatever type of thread you decide to use, be certain to buy at one time sufficient thread of the same dye lot to complete the bedspread you wish to make. It is often impossible to match shades later as dye lots vary.

Since most of the bedspreads in this book are made by crocheting small motifs and then joining these motifs together until the desired size is obtained, the component parts can be used to make a wide variety of other objects, such as scarves, doilies, purses, mantillas, tablecloths, stoles, and so forth.

For perfect results the number of stitches and rows should correspond with that indicated in the directions. Before starting your bedspread, make a small sample of the stitch, working with the suggested needle size and desired thread. If your working tension is too tight or too loose, use a coarser or finer crochet hook to obtain the correct gauge.

When you have completed your bedspread, it should be washed and blocked before using. No matter how carefully you have worked, blocking will improve the spread's appearance and give it a "professional" look. Use a good neutral soap or detergent and make suds in warm water. Wash by squeezing the suds through the bedspread, but do not rub. Rinse two or three times in clear water and squeeze out the excess water. Following the measurements given with the pattern, and using rust proof pins, pin the article right side down on a well-padded, flat surface. Be sure to pin out all picots, loops, scallops, etc., along the outside edges. When the spread is almost completely dry, press through a damp cloth with a moderately hot iron (do not rest the iron on the decorative raised stitches). When thoroughly dry, remove pins.

All of the stitches and the abbreviations used in the projects in this book are explained on page 48.

Keepsake

MATERIALS:

SINGLE SIZE
J. & P. COATS BEDSPREAD COTTON
16 balls of White or Ecru.

DOUBLE SIZE
J. & P. COATS BEDSPREAD COTTON
21 balls of White or Ecru.

MILWARD'S STEEL CROCHET HOOK No. 7 or 8.

GAUGE:

7 bls or sps make 2 inches; 7 rows make 2 inches. Each block measures about 9 inches square. For a single size spread about 71 x 107 inches, including 4-inch fringe all around, make 7 x 11 blocks. For double size spread, about 89 x 107 inches, including 4-inch fringe, make 9 x 11 blocks.

BLOCK . . . Ch 12, join with sl st. **1st rnd:** Ch 8, d c in same place as sl st (corner made), (ch 2, skip 2 ch, in next ch make d c, ch 5, and d c) 3 times; ch 2, skip 2 ch, sl st in 3rd st of ch-8. **2nd rnd:** Ch 3, * 2 d c in corner sp, d c in 3rd ch of same corner, ch 5, d c in same ch as last d c (corner made); 2 d c in same corner sp, d c in next d c, ch 2, d c in next d c. Repeat from * around, ending with ch 2, sl st in 3rd ch of ch-3. **3rd rnd:** Ch 3, d c in next 3 d c, * 2 d c in corner sp, d c in center ch of same corner (2 bls made); ch 5, d c in same place as last d c, 2 d c in same sp, d c in next 4 d c, 2 d c in next sp, d c in next 4 d c. Repeat from * around. Join to 3rd ch of ch-3. **4th rnd:** Ch 3, d c in next 3 d c (bl made over bl); * ch 2, skip 2 d c, d c in next d c (sp made over bl); 2 d c in corner sp, d c in center ch of same corner,

ch 5, d c in same place, 2 d c in same corner sp, d c in next d c, ch 2, skip 2 d c, d c in next 10 d c. Repeat from * around, ending with d c in last 6 d c. Join. **5th rnd:** Ch 5, skip 2 d c, d c in next d c (sp made over bl); ch 2, d c in next d c (sp made over sp); make another sp, * 2 d c in corner sp; in center ch of same corner make d c, ch 5, and d c; 2 d c in same corner, d c in next d c, 3 sps, d c in next 3 d c (1 bl made); 3 sps. Repeat from * around, ending with d c in last 3 d c. Join. Ch 5 for beginning of 6th rnd and follow chart for remainder of block, making ch-5 at corners. The 1st sp of 6th rnd is indicated by "X" on chart. Beginning of rnds is indicated on chart by heavy line.

Make necessary number of blocks, and sew together on wrong side with neat over-and-over stitches. Attach thread and work a row of sps all around spread.

FRINGE . . . Cut ten 12-inch strands of thread. Double the strands, forming a loop. Insert hook in corner sp on block and pull loop through; then pull loose ends through loop and pull tight. Make a fringe in every other sp all around. Trim fringe evenly to measure 4 inches. Block to measurements given.

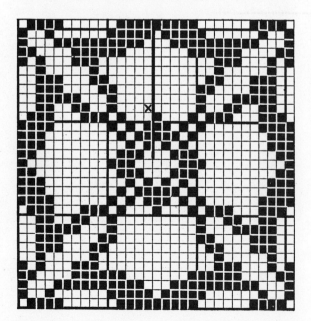

Keepsake

Beautiful filet, patterned with huge blooms in a geometric
pattern, has a delightful colonial feeling in heavy cotton thread. Ex-
travagantly fringed . . . a spread to use . . . to cherish as a keepsake.

Cockle Shells

MATERIALS:

SINGLE SIZE	DOUBLE SIZE
CLARK'S O.N.T. "BRITA-SHEEN"	CLARK'S O.N.T. "BRITA-SHEEN"
30 balls.	*38 balls.*

MILWARD'S STEEL CROCHET HOOK No. 7.

GAUGE:

Each block measures about 6 inches square before blocking. For a single size spread about 72 x 105 inches, make 11 x 16 blocks. For a double size spread about 90 x 105 inches, make 14 x 16 blocks.

FIRST BLOCK . . . Starting at center, ch 8. Join with sl st. **1st rnd:** Ch 3, 3 d c in ring, (ch 4, 4 d c in ring) 3 times; ch 4, sl st in top of ch-3 first made. **2nd rnd:** Ch 3, * d c in next d c, d c in each d c to sp; in sp make 3 d c, ch 4 and 3 d c (corner). Repeat from * around, ending with sl st in top of ch-3. **3rd, 4th and 5th rnds:** Repeat 2nd rnd. **6th rnd:** Ch 3, d c in next 3 d c, ch 4, skip 4 d c, d c in next 4 d c, * ch 4, in corner sp make 3 d c, ch 4 and 3 d c; (ch 4, skip 4 d c, d c in next 4 d c) 3 times. Repeat from * around, ending with ch 4, sl st in top of ch-3. **7th rnd:** Sl st in next 3 d c, sl st in sp, ch 3, 3 d c in same sp, ch 4, skip 4 d c, 4 d c in next sp, * ch 4, in corner sp make 3 d c, ch 4 and 3 d c; (ch 4, 4 d c in next sp) 4 times. Repeat from * around, ending as before. **8th rnd:** Sl st in next 3 d c and in next sp, ch 3, 3 d c in same sp, ch 4, 4 d c in next sp, * ch 4, in corner sp make 3 d c, ch 4 and 3 d c, (ch 4, 4 d c in next sp) 5 times. Repeat from * around, ending as before. **9th rnd:** Ch 3, d c in next 3 d c, ch 4, s c in next 4 d c, * ch 4, in corner sp make 12 d c, (ch 4, s c in next 4 d c, ch 4, d c in next 4 d c) twice; ch 4, s c in next 4 d c. Repeat from * around, ending as before. **10th and 11th rnds:** Ch 3, d c in next 3 d c, ch 4, s c in next 4 s c, * ch 4, (d c in next d c, ch 1) 11 times; d c in next d c, (ch 4, s c in next 4 s c, ch 4, d c in next 4 d c) twice; ch 4, s c in next 4 s c. Repeat from * around, ending as before. **12th rnd:** Ch 3, d c in next 3 d c, ch 4, s c in next 4 s c, ** ch 4, * s c in next d c, ch 4, s c in 4th ch from hook (a p made); s c in next sp. Repeat from * 10 more times; s c in next d c, p, s c in same place as last s c, (ch 4, s c in next 4 s c, ch 4, d c in next 4 d c) twice; ch 4, s c in next 4 s c. Repeat from ** around, ending as before. Fasten off.

SECOND BLOCK . . . Work as for First Block to 11th rnd incl. **12th rnd:** Work as for 12th rnd of First Block until 8th p is completed, work s c in next sp, s c in next d c, ch 2, s c in corresponding p of 1st block, ch 2, s c in 2nd ch from joining (thus joining corresponding p's); s c in sp, and continue rnd as for First Block, joining next 3 p's and first 4 p's of next corner to corresponding p's of First Block. Sew corresponding d c-scallops with neat over-and-over stitches, as in illustration.

Make necessary number of blocks, joining adjacent sides as Second Block was joined to First, leaving 4 center p's at each corner free. Block to measurements given.

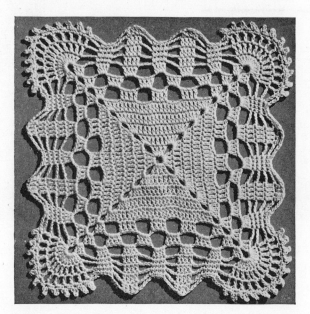

Cockle Shells

Perfectionism in a spread, for it's at home in practically every type room. The large squares have a smart, austere simplicity . . . but the cockle shells that blithely round the corners give it a lighthearted theme.

Fair and Square

MATERIALS: Use one of the following threads:

CLARK'S O.N.T. LUSTERSHEEN, *35 skeins of White or Ecru, or 46 skeins of any color for single size spread; 40 skeins of White or Ecru, or 53 skeins of any color for double size spread.*

J. & P. COATS KNIT-CRO-SHEEN, *46 balls of White or Ecru, or 56 balls of any color for single size spread; 53 balls of White or Ecru, or 64 balls of any color for double size spread.*

MILWARD'S *steel crochet hook No. 9.*

GAUGE: Each block measures 6¼ inches square. For a double size spread, about 90 x 108 inches, make 14 x 17 blocks. For a single size spread, about 75 x 108 inches, make 12 x 17 blocks.

BLOCK... Starting at center, ch 8, join with sl st. **1st rnd:** Ch 3, 15 d c in ring. Join to 3rd st of ch-3 first made. **2nd rnd:** * Ch 5, skip 1 d c, s c in next d c. Repeat from * around. **3rd rnd:** In each loop make s c, half d c, 3 d c, half d c, s c (8 petals). **4th rnd:** Sl st to 2nd d c of 1st petal, * ch 8, d c in 4th ch from hook,

ch 1, skip 1 ch, d c in next ch, ch 2, make s c where ch-8 started, ch 8, s c in 2nd d c of next petal. Repeat from * around, ending with ch 4, tr where 1st ch-8 started. **5th rnd:** S c in loop, ch 4, 2 tr in same loop, holding back the last loop of each tr on hook; thread over and draw through all loops on hook (a cluster); * make 11 tr in sp at tip of next ch-8, 3 tr in next ch-8 loop, holding back the last loop of each tr on hook; thread over and draw through all loops (another cluster). Repeat from * around, joining last tr to tip of 1st cluster made. **6th rnd:** Ch 12 (to count as tr and ch-8), * skip 5 tr, s c in next tr, ch 8, tr at tip of next cluster, ch 8. Repeat from * around, ending with ch 8, sl st in 4th st of ch-12 first made. **7th rnd:** 10 s c in each sp around. Join. **8th rnd:** Ch 3, d c in each st around. Join. **9th rnd:** Ch 8 (to count as d c and ch-5), skip 4 d c, half d c in next d c, ch 5, skip 4 d c, * s c in next d c, ch 5, skip 4 d c, half d c in next d c, ch 5, skip 4 d c, d c in next d c, ch 5, skip 9 d c, in next d c make 3 tr with ch-5 between; ch 5, skip 9 d c, d c in next d c, ch 5, skip 4 d c, half d c in next d c, ch 5, skip 4 d c. Repeat from * around, ending with ch 5, sl st in 3rd st of ch-8 first made. **10th rnd:** Ch 8, s c in next half d c, 5 s c in next sp, * s c in next s c, 5 s c in next sp, s c in next half d c, ch 5, d c in next d c, ch 5, tr in next tr; in next tr make 3 tr with ch-5 between; tr in next tr, ch 5, d c in next d c, ch 5, s c in next half d c, 5 s c in next sp. Repeat from * around, ending with ch 5, sl st in 3rd st of ch-8 first made. **11th rnd:** Ch 5 (to count as d c and ch-2); * skip 2 sts, d c in next st, ch 2. Repeat from * around, making d c, ch 5, d c in each corner tr. Join. **12th rnd:** Ch 1, * 2 s c in next sp, s c in next d c. Repeat from * around, making 3 s c, ch 3, 3 s c in corner sp. Join. **13th rnd:** Ch 3, d c in each st around, making 5 d c in each corner sp. Join and fasten off.

Make necessary number of blocks and sew together on wrong side, with neat over-and-over stitches.

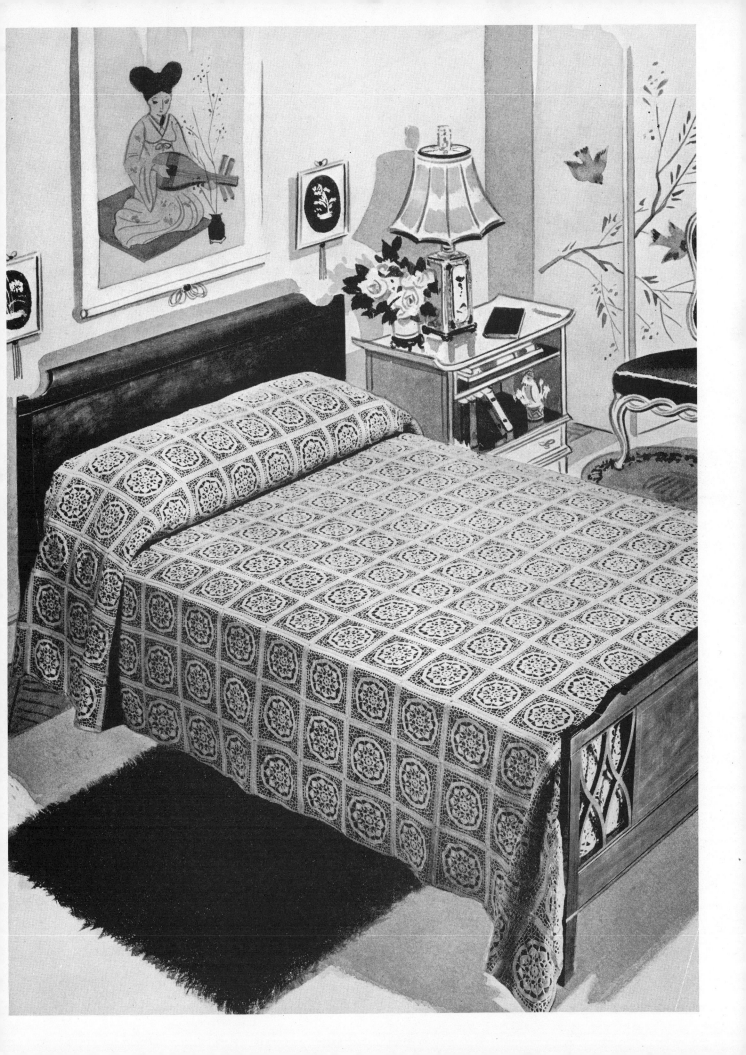

Irish Melody

MATERIALS:

SINGLE SIZE
J. & P. COATS KNIT-CRO-SHEEN
53 balls of White or Ecru,
or 84 balls of any color.

DOUBLE SIZE
J. & P. COATS KNIT-CRO-SHEEN
67 balls of White or Ecru,
or 106 balls of any color.

MILWARD'S STEEL CROCHET HOOK No. 7.

GAUGE:

Each motif measures about 5 inches from one pc st edge to opposite edge, across center before blocking. For a single size spread about 70 x 105 inches, make 292 motifs. For a double size spread about 88 x 105 inches, make 370 motifs.

MOTIF . . . Starting at center, ch 8. Join with sl st. **1st rnd:** 12 s c in ring. Sl st in 1st s c made. **2nd rnd:** Ch 6, skip 1 s c, * d c in next s c, ch 3. Repeat from * around. Sl st in 3rd st of ch-6 first made (6 sps). **3rd rnd:** In each ch-3 sp around, make s c, half d c, 5 d c, half d c and s c (6 petals). **4th rnd:** * Ch 5, s c in next d c between petals (working from behind petals). Repeat from * around, ending with ch 5, sl st in 3rd st of ch-6 on 2nd rnd. **5th rnd:** In each ch-5 loop around, make s c, half d c, d c, 5 tr, d c, half d c and s c (6 large petals). **6th rnd:** Sl st to center st of next petal, ch 6, d c in same place as last sl st, * ch 5, d c between petals, ch 5, in center st of next petal, make d c, ch 3 and d c. Repeat from * around, ending with ch 5, sl st to 3rd st of ch-6 first made. **7th rnd:** * In next ch-3 sp make s c, half d c, 5 d c, half d c and s c (petal made); ch 5, pc st in next d c—*to make a pc st ch 1, 5 d c in same place, drop loop from hook, insert hook in ch preceding 5 d c and draw dropped loop through;* ch 5. Repeat from * around, ending with ch 5, sl st in 1st s c made. **8th rnd:** Sl st to center st of next petal, ch 6, d c in same place as last sl st, * ch 5, pc st in next sp, ch 1, pc st in next sp, ch 5, in center st of next petal make d c, ch 3 and d c. Repeat from * around, ending rnd with ch 5, sl st in 3rd st of ch-6 first made.

9th rnd: * In next ch-3 sp make a petal as before, ch 5, pc st in next sp, ch 1, pc st in sp between pc sts, ch 1, pc st in next sp, ch 5. Repeat from * around, ending with ch 5, sl st in 1st s c made. **10th rnd:** Sl st to center st of petal, ch 6, d c in same place as last sl st, * ch 5, pc st in next sp, (ch 1, pc st in next sp) 3 times; ch 5, in center st of next petal make d c, ch 3 and d c. Repeat from * around, ending with ch 5, sl st in 3rd st of ch-6 first made. **11th rnd:** * In next ch-3 sp make a petal, ch 5, pc st in next sp, (ch 1, pc st in next sp) 4 times; ch 5. Repeat from * around, ending with ch 5, sl st in 1st s c made. **12th rnd:** S c in same

place as sl st, * (ch 4, skip 1 st, s c in next st) 4 times; ch 4, pc st in next sp, (ch 1, pc st in next sp) 5 times; ch 4, s c in next s c. Repeat from * around, ending with ch 4, sl st in 1st s c made.

Make necessary number of motifs, sewing adjacent pc st edges as in illustration with neat over-and-over stitches.

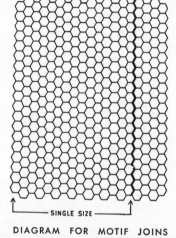

DIAGRAM FOR MOTIF JOINS

Irish Melody

A darlin'—this leaf and flower fantasy . . . to test
the skill of your crochet hook. Always incredibly lovely, this Irish
Crochet has a smart embossed surface delightful in any room.

11

This design delves into the mellow Colonial past to endow modern rooms of old fashioned charm with the authentic zigzag popcorn pattern.

Past and Present

MATERIALS: J. & P. Coats Bedspread Cotton, *White or Ecru, 25 balls for single size spread, about 72 x 108 inches; 31 balls for double size spread, about 89 x 108 inches.*

Milward's *steel crochet hook No. 5.*

Gauge: 9 d c make 1 inch; 3 rows make 1 inch.

FIRST STRIP... Starting at one side, ch 688 (9 ch sts to 1 inch) for single size, or ch 884 for double size. **1st row:** D c in 4th and 5th chains from hook, leaving the last loop of each d c on hook; thread over and draw through all loops on hook (a decrease); d c in next 2 ch, leaving the last loop of each d c on hook; thread over and draw through all loops on hook (another decrease); d c in next 44 ch, ch 4, d c in next 47 ch. * Skip 4 ch, d c in next 47 ch, ch 4, d c in next 47 ch. Repeat from * across, ending with d c in 45 ch (d c in next 2 ch, leaving the last loop of each d c on hook; thread over and draw through all loops on hook) twice—2 d c decreased. Fasten off. Hereafter pick up only the back loop of each st throughout spread. **2nd row:** Attach thread to 3rd st of turning ch at beginning of previous row, ch 3, (make a d c in each of next 2 sts, leaving the last loop of each d c on hook; thread over and draw through all loops on hook) twice. * Pc st in next st—*to make a pc st, ch 1, make 5 d c in st, remove hook, insert hook back in ch-1 and draw dropped loop through.* ** D c in next 3 d c. Repeat from * until 11 pc sts are made. D c in next d c, d c in next 2 ch, ch 4, d c in next 2 ch, d c in next d c; (pc st in next d c, d c in next 3 d c) 11 times; skip 4 d c. Repeat from ** across, decreasing 2 d c at end of row as before. Fasten off. **3rd row:** Attach thread to 3rd st of ch-3 at beginning of previous row, ch 3, dec. 2 sts as before, d c in next 44 sts, ch 4, d c in next 47 sts, * skip 4 sts, d c in next 47 sts, ch 4, d c in next 47 sts. Repeat from * across, decreasing 2 sts at end of row as before. Fasten off. Repeat 2nd and 3rd rows alternately until piece measures 21 inches, ending with a pc-st row. This completes one

strip. Make 3 more strips like this and sew each strip to previous one with neat over-and-over stitches on wrong side *(if desired, bedspread may be made in one piece by continuing to work first strip until piece measures 84 inches. Then follow directions for "FILL-IN BETWEEN SCALLOPS" and "BORDER").*

Now make another strip, ending with a d c-row. Fasten off. Attach thread to 3rd st of ch-3 of previous row, ch 3, dec. 2 sts as before, d c in each st across to within 4 sts of ch-4, dec. 2 sts. Fasten off. **Next row:** Attach thread to 3rd st of ch-3 of previous row, ch 3, dec. 2 sts; (pc st in next st, d c in next 3 sts) 9 times; pc st in next st, d c in next 2 sts, dec. 2 sts. Fasten off. Alternate the last 2 rows, always decreasing 2 sts at both ends of each row, until piece graduates into a point (2 pc sts less in each pc-st row).

FILL-IN BETWEEN SCALLOPS...1st row: Skip the ch-4 of point, attach thread to 1st d c, ch 3, dec. 3 sts, d c in next 2 d c; (pc st in next d c, d c in next 3 d c) 9 times, skip 4 sts; (d c in next 3 d c, pc st in next d c) 9 times; d c in next 2 d c, dec. 3 sts. Fasten off. **2nd row:** Attach thread to ch-3 of previous row, ch 3, dec. 3 sts, d c in each st to within center 4 d c, skip these 4 d c, d c in each st to within last 6 sts, dec. 3 sts and fasten off. Continue in this manner until 2 pc sts remain in the last pc-st row. **Next row:** Repeat 2nd row. **Following row:** Attach thread to ch-3 of previous row, ch 3, dec. 2 sts, d c in next st, skip 4 sts, d c in next st, dec. 2 sts. Ch 1, turn. Sl st in 1st st. Fasten off. Fill in all spaces between scallops in this manner (this is lower edge of spread).

BORDER...1st row: Attach thread to 1st st of one side, ch 3, d c in next 2 sts, * pc st in next st, d c in next 3 sts. Repeat from * across. Fasten off. **2nd row:** Attach thread to 3rd st of ch-3 of previous row and make d c in each st across. Fasten off. Alternate these 2 rows until border measures 6 inches, ending with a pc-st row. Work other border in same way.

12

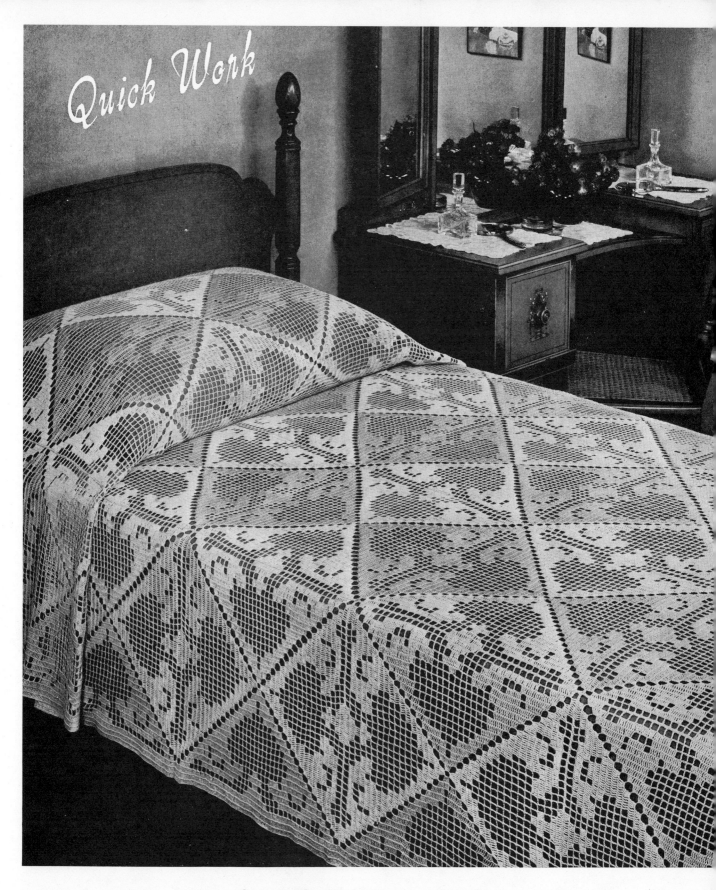

Quick Work

A square a day's the idea for this one . . . and it's fun to do, for nimble fingers make this work go like magic. A spread with serene, lady-like distinction in its large scale baroque filet design.

Quick Work

MATERIALS:

CLARK'S BIG BALL MERCERIZED CROCHET, *size 10*

SINGLE SIZE	DOUBLE SIZE
32 balls of White or Ecru.	*38 balls of White or Ecru.*

MILWARD'S STEEL CROCHET HOOK *No. 5.*

GAUGE:

(When blocked) 2 sps make 1 inch; 2 rows make 1 inch. Each block measures about 18 inches square after blocking. For a single size spread, about 74 x 110 inches, including edging, make 4 x 6 blocks. For a double size spread about 92 x 110 inches, including edging, make 5 x 6 blocks.

BLOCK . . . Starting at center, ch 11, join with sl st to form a ring. **1st rnd:** Ch 4 (to count as tr), 4 tr in ring, * ch 7, 5 tr in ring. Repeat from * 2 more times; ch 7. Join with sl st to top of ch-4. **2nd rnd:** Ch 4, tr in next 4 tr, * 4 tr in sp, ch 7, 4 tr in same sp, tr in next 5 tr. Repeat from * around. Join. **3rd rnd:** Ch 7, * skip 3 tr, tr in next 5 tr, in corner sp make 4 tr, ch 7 and 4 tr; make tr in next 5 tr, ch 3. Repeat from * around. Join to 4th ch of ch-7. **4th rnd:** Ch 7, * tr in next 9 tr, in corner sp make 4 tr, ch 7 and 4 tr; make tr in next 9 tr, ch 3. Repeat from * around. Join. **5th rnd:** Ch 7, tr in next tr, * ch 3, skip 3 tr, tr in next 9 tr, in corner sp make 4 tr, ch 7 and 4 tr; tr in next 9 tr, ch 3, skip 3 tr, tr in next tr (sp made over bl), ch 3, tr in next tr. Repeat from * around. Join.

Beginning with 6th rnd, follow chart until 13 rnds in all are completed. The first sp of 6th rnd is indicated by "X." **14th rnd:** Ch 4, 3 tr in sp, tr in next tr (bl made over sp), ch 3, and continue to follow chart to complete rnd. Starting with 15th rnd, follow chart to complete block. Make necessary number of blocks and sew together on wrong side with neat over-and-over stitches.

EDGING . . . Attach thread, ch 4, and work 3 rnds of tr, making corners as on blocks and being careful edging does not ruffle. Block to measurements given.

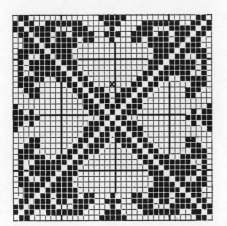

Land o' Cotton

An allover diagonal popcorn pattern. The "puffs" are smartly oversized and the grand marshmallow texture looks for all the world like a field of fluffy white cotton blossoms! Try pastels for a smart effect.

Land o' Cotton

MATERIALS:

SINGLE SIZE
J. & P. COATS KNIT-CRO-SHEEN
60 balls of White or Ecru,
or 96 balls of any color.

DOUBLE SIZE
J. & P. COATS KNIT-CRO-SHEEN
75 balls of White or Ecru,
or 120 balls of any color.

CRIB SIZE
J. & P. COATS KNIT-CRO-SHEEN
23 balls of White or Ecru,
or 36 balls of any color.

MILWARD'S STEEL CROCHET HOOK No. 7.

GAUGE:

8 d c make 1 inch. When completed, single size spread measures
72 x 108 inches; double size spread measures 90 x 108 inches;
crib size spread measures 45 x 60 inches.

Starting at bottom, make a chain (8 ch sts to 1 inch) 2¼ yards long for single size spread; 2¾ yards long for double size spread; or 1½ yards long for crib size spread. **1st row:** D c in 4th ch from hook, d c in next ch (3 d c, counting the turning ch). Make a pc st as follows: * Ch 1, 9 tr in next ch, drop loop from hook, insert hook in the ch-1 preceding the 9 tr and draw dropped loop through; then make d c in next 7 ch. Repeat from * across, until row measures 67 inches for single size (83 inches for double size, or 42 inches for crib size), ending with 3 d c (1 pc-st row made). Cut off remaining chain. Ch 1, turn. **2nd row:** S c in 1st 3 sts, * insert hook in back of pc st and in center tr of same pc st, draw loop through and finish as for an s c. Make s c in next 7 d c. Repeat from * across, ending with s c in top st of turning ch. Ch 3, turn. **3rd row:** D c in next (2nd) s c and the following 3 s c, pc st in next s c, * d c in next 7 s c, pc st in next s c. Repeat from * across, ending with d c in last 9 s c. Ch 1, turn. **4th row:** S c in each st across, working over pc sts as before, ending with s c in top of turning ch. Ch 3, turn. **5th row:** D c in next (2nd) s c and in following 5 s c, * pc st in next s c, d c in next 7 s c. Repeat from * across, ending with d c in last 7 s c. Ch 1, turn. **6th row:** Same as 4th row. **7th row:** D c in next (2nd) s c and the following 7 s c, * pc st in next s c, d c in next 7 s c. Repeat from * across, ending with d c in last 5 s c. Ch 1, turn. **8th row:** Same as 4th row. **9th row:** D c in next (2nd) s c and in following s c, * pc st in next s c, d c in next 7 s c. Repeat from * across, ending

with d c in last 3 s c. Ch 1, turn. The 2nd to 9th rows incl. constitute the pattern. Work in pattern until piece measures 104 inches for single or double size spreads (or 58 inches for crib size), ending with the 2nd row of pattern. Fasten off. Block to measurements given.

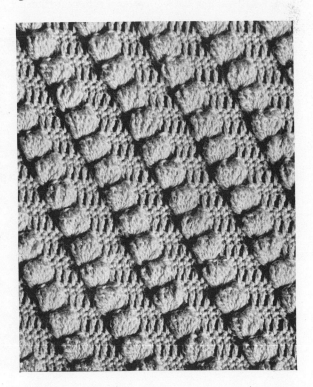

Maker of Dreams

MATERIALS: Use one of the following threads in size 20, White or Ecru:

J. & P. Coats Big Ball Best Six Cord Mercerized Crochet, 39 balls for single size spread, or 48 balls for double size spread.

Clark's O.N.T. Mercerized Crochet, 66 balls for single size spread, or 83 balls for double size spread.

J. & P. Coats Mercerized Crochet, 93 balls for single size spread, or 116 balls for double size spread.

Milward's steel crochet hook No. 9.

Gauge: Each motif measures 4½ inches in diameter, including picots. For a single size spread, about 72 x 108 inches, make 16 x 24 motifs. For a double size spread, about 90 x 108 inches, make 20 x 24 motifs.

FIRST MOTIF... Starting at center, ch 5, 15 d c in 2nd ch made (ch 3 at beginning counts as 1 d c). Join with sl st to top st of ch-3 first made. **2nd rnd:** * Ch 5, skip 1 d c, s c in next d c. Repeat from *

around, ending with sl st at base of ch-5 first made, sl st in each of 1st 3 ch. **3rd rnd:** S c in loop, * ch 6, s c in next loop. Repeat from * around, ending with sl st in 1st s c made and in each of next 3 ch. **4th rnd:** S c in loop, * ch 7, s c in next loop. Repeat from *, ending with sl st at base of 1st ch-7, sl st in loop. **5th rnd:** Ch 3, 8 d c in same loop, 9 d c in each loop around, join. **6th rnd:** Ch 15, sl st in sp between d c-groups. Continue thus around, ending with sl st in 1st sl st. **7th rnd:** Make half d c, 8 d c, ch 3, 8 d c and half d c in loop; s c in sl st. Continue thus around. Sl st across to ch-3 at tip of 1st petal, sl st in ch-3. **8th rnd:** Ch 3, in same sp make 3 d c, ch 1 and 4 d c; * ch 13, in next sp make 4 d c, ch 1 and 4 d c. Repeat from * around, join. **9th rnd:** Sl st in next 3 d c and in ch-1; ch 6 (to count as d c and ch-3), d c in same ch-1; ch 6, in 7th st of ch-13 make d c, ch 3 and d c; ch 6, in ch-1 between d c-groups make d c, ch 3 and d c. Ch 6 and continue thus around, join. **10th rnd:** Ch 7, sl st in 4th ch from hook (p), * in ch-3 loop make 2 d c, ch 4, sl st in top of d c just made (another p); 2 d c, p, d c in d c following ch-3; in ch-6 make half d c, 5 s c and half d c; d c in d c following ch-6, p. Repeat from * around, ending with half d c, join. Fasten off.

SECOND MOTIF... Like 1st motif to 9th rnd incl. **10th rnd:** In ch-3 make ch 7, sl st in 4th ch from hook, 2 d c, ch 2, sl st in corresponding p of 1st motif, ch 2, sl st at top of last d c on motif in work, 2 d c, p, d c in d c. Half d c, 5 s c and half d c in ch-6 sp, d c in d c; p, 2 d c in ch-3; make a p, joining to corresponding p on 1st motif; 2 d c, p, d c in d c, half d c in loop. Complete rnd as for 1st motif (no more joining).

Make necessary number of motifs, joining 2 p's at each side to corresponding p's on adjacent motifs, leaving 2 p-sections free between joinings on each motif.

FILL-IN LACE... Work as for motif to 3rd rnd incl. **4th rnd:** S c in loop, ch 5, drop loop from hook, insert hook in a center p of any free picot section in space between joinings, * draw loop through, ch 5, s c in next loop on motif in work. Ch 5, drop loop from hook and insert it in center p of next free picot section. Repeat from * around, ending with sl st in 1st s c made. Fasten off securely. Fill in all spaces between joinings in this manner.

Through the years the beauty of this spread will endure! The whirl of the motifs matched against filet strips is an exciting study in contrasts.

Heritage

MATERIALS: J. & P. COATS BEDSPREAD COTTON, *11 balls of White or Ecru for single size spread; 15 balls for double size spread.*

MILWARD'S *steel crochet hook No. 7 or 8.*

WHEEL STRIPS

GAUGE: Wheel measures 4½ inches in diameter when blocked. Make 24 wheels for each strip. For single size spread, about 71 x 108 inches, make 9 wheel strips. For double size spread, about 95 x 108 inches, make 12 wheel strips.

WHEEL... Starting at center, ch 8, join with sl st. **1st rnd:** Ch 4 (to count as d c and ch-1), * d c in ring, ch 1. Repeat from * 10 more times, join (12 sps). **2nd rnd:** Sl st in sp, ch 5 (to count as d tr); 2 d tr

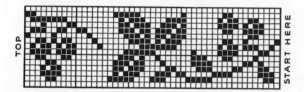

(above) **Chart for Filet Strip**

(below) **Detail of Design**

in sp, holding back the last loop of each st on hook; * thread over and draw through all loops on hook, ch 1 tightly (cluster); ch 5, 3 d tr in next sp, holding back the last loop of each st on hook. Repeat from *, ending with ch 5, join. **3rd rnd:** Ch 1, 2 s c in next loop, ch 16, s c in 2nd ch from hook; * under chain make half d c, 2 d c, 11 tr, 2 d c, half d c, s c (spoke); 2 s c in ch-5 loop, s c at tip of cluster, 2 s c in next loop. Ch 15, drop loop from hook, insert hook in 11th st made on previous spoke and draw loop through, s c under ch-16. Repeat from * to 11th st incl. on ch-16 of 12th spoke; drop loop from hook, insert it at tip of 1st (unconnected) spoke and draw loop through; complete spoke. Complete rnd, join and fasten off.

Make 23 more wheels. Place wheels in a strip, and pin 2 spokes of each to corresponding spokes of adjacent wheels. Sew together neatly at pin-marks, on wrong side. Attach thread to center free st of spoke to right of joining; ch 7, 2 tr tr at base of ch-7, retaining last loop of each st on hook; thread over and draw through all loops on hook; make 3 d tr in center st of next spoke, retaining last loop of each st on hook; thread over and draw through all loops on hook, ch 1 tightly. Fasten off, leaving a 6-inch thread for sewing. Work clusters thus at each free section next to joinings. Make 1 cluster at end wheel of each strip.

FILET STRIPS

GAUGE: 4 sps make 1 inch; 4 rows make 1 inch.

Make 8 strips for single size; make 11 strips for double size.

Starting at bottom, ch 50. **1st row:** D c in 8th ch from hook, ch 2, skip 2 ch, d c in next ch (2 sps); make 4 more sps, d c in next 3 ch (these 4 d c make 1 bl); 8 more sps. Ch 5, turn. **2nd row:** D c in next d c, 2 d c in next sp, d c in next d c, 2 d c in next sp, d c in next d c (1 sp and 2 bls); ch 2, d c in next d c (sp); 3 more sps, 1 bl, 7 more sps. Ch 5, turn. Now follow chart to top, beginning with 3rd row (this completes 1 design). Repeat entire design until strip measures 108 inches (432 rows). Fasten off.

Alternate wheel and filet strips. Sew spokes and clusters of wheel strips to filet strips, as in illustration.

20

Traditional

MATERIALS:

CLARK'S BIG BALL MERCERIZED CROCHET, *size 20*

SINGLE SIZE
34 balls of White or Ecru.

DOUBLE SIZE
43 balls of White or Ecru.

MILWARD'S STEEL CROCHET HOOK *No. 9.*

GAUGE:

Each motif measures about 4¼ inches square when blocked. For a single size spread about 72 x 106 inches, including edging, make 16 x 24 motifs. For a double size spread, about 90 x 106 inches, including edging, make 20 x 24 motifs.

FIRST MOTIF . . . Starting at center, ch 8. Join with sl st. **1st rnd:** Ch 4, 3 tr in ring holding back on hook the last loop of each tr, thread over and draw through all loops on hook, ch 1 to fasten (a 3-tr cluster made), * ch 7, make 4 tr in ring holding back on hook the last loop of each tr, finish cluster. Repeat from * 2 more times; ch 7, sl st in tip of 1st cluster. **2nd rnd:** Ch 4, 3-tr cluster in same place as sl st, * ch 3, 5 tr in next ch-7 sp, ch 4, 4-tr cluster in tip of next cluster. Repeat from * around. Join last ch-4 to tip of 1st cluster. **3rd rnd:** Ch 4, 2-tr cluster in same place as sl st, ch 2, 3-tr cluster in same place, * ch 4, tr in next ch-4 sp, tr in next 5 tr, tr in next sp, ch 4, in tip of next cluster make 3-tr cluster, ch 2 and 3-tr cluster. Repeat from * around. Join last ch-4 to tip of 1st cluster. **4th rnd:** Sl st in ch-2 sp, ch 4, 2-tr cluster in same place as last sl st, in same sp make (ch 2, 3-tr cluster) twice; * ch 3, 5 tr in next ch-4 sp, ch 3, skip 1 tr, tr in next 5 tr holding back on hook the last loop of each tr, finish as for a cluster; ch 3, 5 tr in next ch-4 sp, ch 3, in next corner sp make three 3-tr clusters with ch-2 between each cluster. Repeat from * around. Join. **5th rnd:** Sl st in next ch-2 sp, ch 4, 2-tr cluster in same place as last sl st, ch 2, 3-tr cluster in same place, * ch 5, in next ch-2 sp make two 3-tr clusters with ch 2 between, ch 3, tr in next sp, tr in next 5 tr, tr in next sp, ch 3, tr in tip of next cluster, ch 3, tr in next sp, tr in next 5 tr, tr in next sp, ch 3, in next ch-2 sp make two 3-tr clusters with ch-2 between. Repeat from * around. Join. **6th rnd:** Sl st in next ch-2 sp, ch 4, 2-tr cluster in same place as sl st, ch 2, 3-tr cluster in same place, * ch 2, in next ch-2 sp make 3-tr cluster, ch 5 and 3-tr cluster; ch 2, in next ch-2 sp make two 3-tr clusters with ch-2 between, ch 5, skip 1 tr, tr in next 5 tr holding the last loop of each tr on hook, finish as for a cluster; ch 8, skip 1 tr, and ch 3, s c in next tr, ch 8, skip ch-3 and 1 tr, 5-tr cluster over next 5 tr, ch 5, in next ch-2 sp make two 3-tr clusters with ch-2 between. Repeat from * around. Join. Fasten off.

SECOND MOTIF . . . Work first 5 rnds as for First Motif. **6th rnd:** Sl st in next ch-2 sp, ch 4, 2-tr cluster in same place as sl st, ch 2, 3-tr cluster in same place, ch 2, 3-tr cluster in next sp, ch 2, sl st in corresponding sp of First Motif, ch 2, 3-tr cluster back in same place as last cluster on Second Motif, ch 2, in next ch-2 sp make two 3-tr clusters with ch-2 between, ch 2, sl st in sp of First Motif, ch 2, skip 1 tr, 5 tr cluster over next 5 tr, skip 1 tr, 5-tr cluster over next 5 tr, ch 4, sl st in corresponding sp on First Motif, ch 4, skip next tr and ch 4, s c back in next tr on Second Motif. Join the next loop in the same way. Continue as for 6th rnd of First Motif, joining next corner to First Motif as previous corner was joined. Complete rnd as for First Motif. Make necessary number of motifs, joining adjacent sides as Second Motif was joined to First (whenever 4 corners meet, join 3rd and 4th corners to joining of other corners).

EDGING . . . 1st rnd: Attach thread to tip of 1st cluster on corner motif following a joining, ch 8, tr in tip of next cluster, (ch 4, tr in tip of next cluster) twice, (ch 4, tr in next sp) twice, (ch 4, tr in tip of next cluster) 4 times; ch 4, in center st of corner sp make tr, ch 5 and tr; * (ch 4, tr in tip of next cluster) 4 times, (ch 4, tr in next sp) twice, (ch 4, tr in next cluster) 4 times; ch 4, tr in joining. Repeat from * around, turning corners as 1st corner was turned and joining last ch-4 to 4th st of ch-8 first made. **2nd and 3rd rnds:** Ch 8, * tr in next tr, ch 4. Repeat from * around, making tr, ch-5 and tr in center st of each corner sp. Join as before. **4th rnd:** Ch 4, a 3-tr cluster in same place as sl st, * ch 4, a 4 tr-cluster in next tr. Repeat from * around, making an extra ch-4 and cluster in center st of each corner sp. Join to tip of 1st cluster made. **5th rnd:** Ch 4, 4 tr in same place as sl st, * ch 4, s c in tip of next cluster, ch 4, 5 tr in tip of next cluster. Repeat from * to corner cluster, ch 4, s c in next sp, ch 4, 5 tr in tip of corner cluster, ch 4, s c in next sp, ch 4, 5 tr in tip of next cluster, ch 4, s c in tip of next cluster and continue thus around. Join to 4th st of ch-4 first made. **6th rnd:** Ch 4, a 2 tr-cluster in same place as sl st, * ch 5, skip 1 tr, make a 3-tr cluster in next tr, ch 5, make a 3-tr cluster in each of next 2 tr. Repeat from * around. Join and fasten off. Block to measurements given.

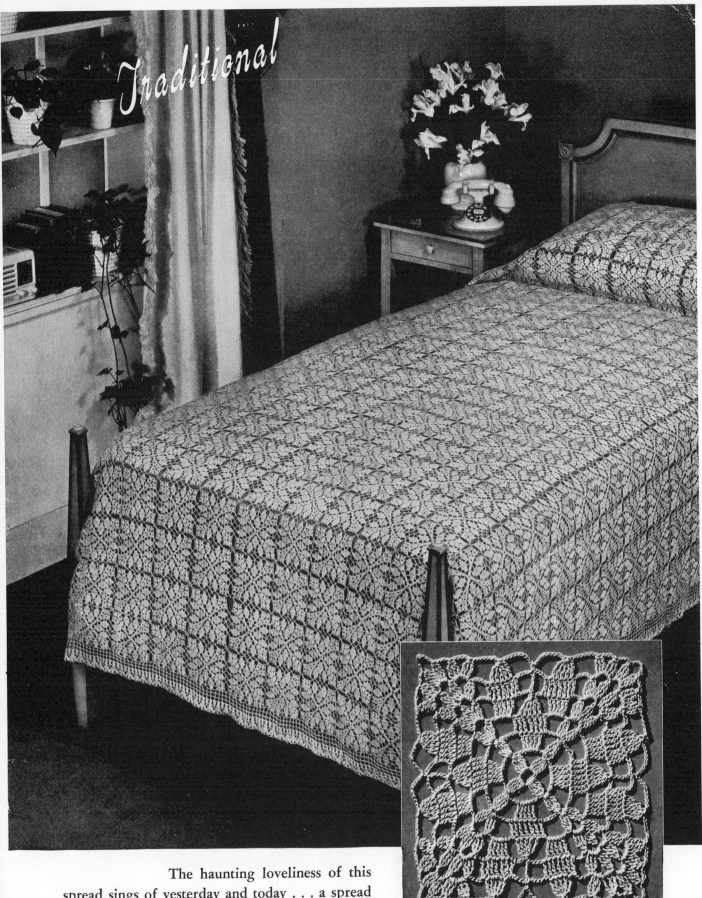

Traditional

The haunting loveliness of this spread sings of yesterday and today . . . a spread like this for your room is a permanent investment in charm.

23

As deliciously feminine as the roses that center each square—this spread in lovely Irish Crochet lace is as sweetly sentimental as a rose garden!

Bed of Roses

MATERIALS: Use one of the following threads: CLARK'S O.N.T. LUSTERSHEEN, *34 skeins of White or Ecru, or 45 skeins of any color for single size spread; 43 skeins of White or Ecru, or 57 skeins of any color for double size spread.*

J. & P. COATS KNIT-CRO-SHEEN, *45 balls of White or Ecru, or 54 balls of any color for single size spread; 57 balls of White or Ecru, or 68 balls of any color for double size spread.*

MILWARD'S *steel crochet hook No. 5 or 6.*

GAUGE: Each block measures 6¼ inches square. For a single size spread, about 72 x 108 inches, make 11 x 17 blocks. For a double size spread, about 92 x 108 inches, make 14 x 17 blocks.

BLOCK...Ch 8, join with sl st. **1st rnd:** Ch 6, * d c in ring, ch 3. Repeat from * 4 more times. Join to 3rd st of ch-6 (6 sps). **2nd rnd:** In each sp make s c, half d c, 2 d c, half d c and s c (6 petals). **3rd rnd:** * Ch 4, s c in d c of 1st rnd (between petals). Repeat from * around. Ch 4, join. **4th rnd:** In each loop make s c, half d c, 3 d c, half d c and s c. **5th rnd:** * Ch 5, s c in back loop of s c of 3rd rnd. Repeat from * around. **6th rnd:** Same as 4th rnd, making 4 d c instead of 3 d c. **7th rnd:** Same as 5th rnd, making ch-6 loops. **8th rnd:** Same as 4th rnd, making 6 d c instead of 3 d c. **9th rnd:** * Ch 3, s c between

3rd and 4th d c at back of next petal, ch 3, s c in back loop of next s c. Repeat from * around. Sl st in 1st ch-3 loop. **10th rnd:** Ch 3, 3 d c in same place as sl st, * ch 2, 4 d c in next sp. Repeat from * around; join. **11th rnd:** Sl st in next 3 d c, sl st in sp, ch 3, d c in same sp; * (ch 5, s c in 4th ch from hook, thus making a p) 3 times; s c in ch between 1st 2 p's, p, ch 1, s c in ch between 1st p and last d c, 2 d c in same sp as last d c, ch 3, 2 d c in next ch-2 sp. Repeat from * around, ending with 2 d c in same place as last d c, ch 3, sl st in 3rd st of ch-3 first made. Fasten off. **12th rnd:** Attach thread between 2nd and 3rd p's of 1st p-loop, * ch 11, s c between 2nd and 3rd p's of next p-loop. Repeat from * around. **13th rnd:** S c in each ch and in each s c around. Ch 1, turn. Work is now done in rows instead of rnds, picking up only the back loop of each s c.

1st row: Sl st in 1st s c, s c in next 35 s c. Ch 2, turn. **2nd row:** Skip 2 s c, s c in next 15 s c, pc st in next s c—*to make a pc st, ch 1, make 5 d c in st, remove hook, insert hook back in ch-1 and draw dropped loop through, ch 1 to fasten.* S c in next 15 s c. Ch 2, turn. **3rd row:** Skip 2 s c, s c in each st across. Ch 2, turn. **4th row:** Skip 2 s c, s c in next 11 s c, pc st in next s c, s c in next 3 s c, pc st in next s c, s c in next 11 s c. Ch 2, turn. **5th row:** Same as 3rd row. **6th row:** Skip 3 s c, s c in next 6 s c, pc st in next s c; (s c in next 3 s c, pc st in next s c) twice; s c in next 7 s c. Ch 2, turn. **7th row:** Same as 3rd row, but skip 3 s c (instead of 2 s c). **8th row:** Skip 3 s c, s c in next 5 s c, pc st in next st, s c in next 3 s c, pc st in next s c, s c in next 6 s c. Ch 2, turn. **9th row:** Same as 7th row. **10th row:** Skip 3 s c, s c in next 4 s c, pc st in next s c, s c in next 5 s c. Ch 2, turn. **11th row:** Skip 2 s c, s c in next 6 s c. Ch 5, turn. **12th row:** Skip 5 s c, s c in next s c. Fasten off. With wrong side of work toward you, skip s c at tip of p-loop, attach thread and work over next 35 s c. Turn and work as for first corner. Continue in this manner until 4 corners are made. Fasten off. Now work in rnds as follows:

1st rnd: Attach thread in corner loop, ch 5, d c in same loop, ch 2, d c in same loop. * (Ch 3, d c in next turning ch) 4 times; ch 3, tr in next turning ch, ch 3, d tr in s c directly above p-loop, ch 3, tr in next turning ch; (ch 3, d c in next turning ch) 4 times; ch 3, in corner ch-5 loop make d c, ch 2, d c, ch 2 and d c. Repeat from * around. Join last ch-2 to 3rd st of ch-5 first made. **2nd rnd:** Ch 3, d c in next 2 ch, 3 d c in next d c, d c in each st around, making 3 d c in center d c at corners. Fasten off.

Make necessary number of blocks and sew together on wrong side with neat over-and-over stitches.

Rhythm

MATERIALS: J. & P. Coats Bedspread Cotton, *17 balls of White or Ecru for single size spread; 22 balls for double size spread.*

Milward's *steel crochet hook No. 9.*

Gauge: Each block measures 6 inches square. For a single size spread, about 74 x 110 inches including fringe, make 11 x 17 blocks. For a double size spread, about 92 x 110 inches including fringe, make 14 x 17 blocks.

BLOCK...1st rnd: Starting at center, ch 5; 15 d c in 2nd ch made (16 d c in all). Join with sl st to top of 1st d c. **2nd rnd:** Ch 8, d c in same place as sl st (corner); * ch 2, ** skip 1 st, d c in next st. Repeat from * once, ch 5, d c in same place (corner), ch 2. Repeat from ** around, ending with ch 2, join. **3rd rnd:** Ch 3 (to count as d c), d c in each of next 3 ch, ch 5, d c in same ch as last d c was made, d c in next 2 ch, 10 more d c across to next corner ch, ch 5 for corner. Continue thus around, join. **4th rnd:** Ch 4 (to count as s c and ch-3), d c in last d c preceding ch-5, d c in next 3 ch, ch 5, d c in same ch as last d c was made and in next 2 ch, d c in next d c, * ch 3, skip 2 sts, s c in next st, ch 3, skip 2 sts, d c in next st (lacet made). Repeat from * once, d c in next 2 ch; in next ch make d c, ch 5 and d c; d c in next 2 ch,

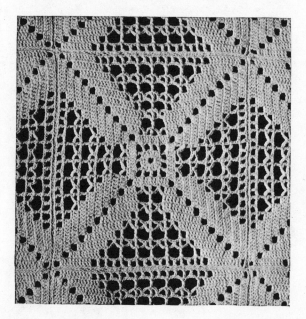

d c in next d c, ch 3. Continue thus around, ending with ch 3, join to 1st ch of ch-4 first made. **5th rnd:** Sl st to top of ch-4, ch 3, d c in each st to within center ch of corner ch-5 (6 d c); in corner ch make d c, ch 5, d c; d c in next 2 ch, d c in next 4 d c, ch 5, d c in d c between lacets (bar); ch 5, d c in next 4 d c and in next 3 ch. Ch 5 and continue thus around, ending with ch 5, join. **6th rnd:** Ch 3, d c in each st to corner ch, inc. in corner ch as before, d c in next 2 ch and across following d c's; * ch 3, s c in center ch of bar, ch 3, d c in d c. Repeat from * once, d c across to corner ch, ch 5. Continue thus around, ending with ch 3, join. **7th rnd:** Ch 5 (to count as d c and ch-2); * skip 2 d c, d c in remaining d c's to corner ch, inc. at corner as before, d c in following 2 ch and in next 7 d c, ch 2, skip 2 d c, d c in next d c, ch 5; skip lacet, d c in next d c; ch 5, d c in next d c after next lacet, ch 2. Repeat from * around, ending with ch 5, join to 3rd st of ch-5. **8th rnd:** Ch 6, s c in d c following ch-2, ch 3, skip 2 sts, d c across to corner ch; inc. at corner, d c across 2 ch and next 7 d c, * ch 3, skip 2 sts, s c in next st; ch 3, skip 2 sts, d c in next d c. Repeat from * 3 more times (4 lacets), d c across to next corner. Continue thus around, ending with ch 3, join. **9th rnd:** Ch 8 (to count as d c and bar), d c in d c following lacet, ch 2, skip 2 d c, d c in next d c; now work as for 7th rnd, having 4 bars and a ch-2 sp at each end, in each group. End with bar, join to 3rd st of ch-8. **10th rnd:** Work as for 8th rnd, beginning with a lacet over bar and having 6 (instead of 4) lacets in each group. End with ch 3, join. **11th rnd:** Work as for 9th rnd, having 6 bars in each group. **12th rnd:** Ch 5, skip 2 sts, d c in next st, ch 2, skip 2 sts, d c in next st (2 sps). Make 2 ch-2 sps over each bar, ch-2 sp over ch-2 sp; at each corner make 10 d c, ch 5 and 10 d c, as before. Fasten off.

Make necessary number of motifs and sew together on wrong side with neat over-and-over stitches.

FRINGE... Make fringe in each ch-2 sp along each edge, except at corners of motifs as follows: Cut 5 strands, each 12 inches long. Double these strands, forming a loop. Pull loop through first sp and draw loose ends through loop. Pull tight. When fringe has been made along 4 sides, trim evenly.

Maker of Magic

MATERIALS:

CLARK'S O.N.T. or J. & P. COATS BIG BALL BEST SIX CORD MERCERIZED CROCHET, *size 20*

SINGLE SIZE	DOUBLE SIZE
62 balls of White or Ecru.	*80 balls of White or Ecru.*

MILWARD'S STEEL CROCHET HOOK No. 9 or 10.

GAUGE:

Each motif measures 3¼ inches in diameter after blocking. For a single size spread about 68 x 105 inches, make 21 x 32 motifs. For a double size spread about 88 x 105 inches, make 27 x 32 motifs.

MOTIF . . . Ch 7, join with sl st to form a ring. **1st rnd:** Ch 3, 15 d c in ring. Join with sl st to top of ch-3. **2nd rnd:** Ch 7, skip 1 d c, * d c in next d c, ch 4. Repeat from * around, joining last ch-3 with sl st to 3rd st of ch 7 (8 sps). **3rd rnd:** Sl st in sp, ch 3, 7 d c in same sp, 8 d c in each following sp around. Join with sl st to top of ch-3. Hereafter pick up only back loop of each d c. **4th rnd:** Ch 3, d c in next 7 d c, * ch 1, d c in next 8 d c. Repeat from * around, ending with ch 1, sl st in top of ch-3. **5th rnd:** Ch 3, d c in next 7 d c, * ch 4, s c in 4th ch from hook (p made), ch 1, d c in next 8 d c. Repeat from * around. Join. **6th rnd:** Ch 3, d c in next 7 d c, * ch 1, a ch-4 p, ch 2, d c in next 8 d c. Repeat from * around. Join. **7th rnd:** Ch 3, d c in next 7 d c, * ch 8, d c in next 8 d c. Repeat from * around. Join. **8th rnd:** Ch 3, d c in next 7 d c, * 12 d c in sp, d c in next 8 d c.

Repeat from * around. Join and fasten off.

Make necessary number of motifs and sew one group of 8 d c of adjacent motifs with neat over-and-over stitches, picking up only the back loop of each st. There will be one group of 8 d c free on each motif between joinings.

FILL-IN MOTIF . . . Repeat first 3 rnds of large motif. Fasten off. Sew group of 8 d c between joinings on each large motif to 8 d c of fill-in motif. Fill all spaces between joinings in same way.

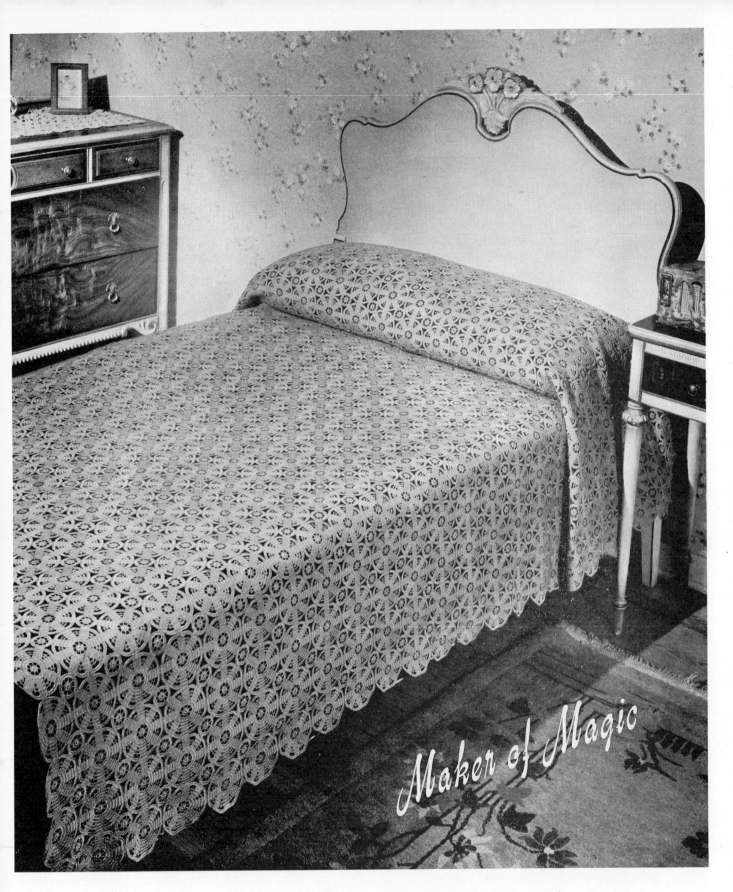

Maker of Magic

Now you see a sailor's wheel . . . now it's a square . . .
for this spread is so ingeniously contrived that square and wheel play
at illusion as they gracefully merge to endow it with unusual beauty.

Dawn o' Day

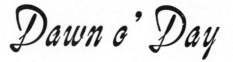

MATERIALS:

CLARK'S O.N.T. or J. & P. COATS BIG BALL BEST SIX CORD MERCERIZED CROCHET, *size 20*

SINGLE SIZE	**DOUBLE SIZE**
41 balls of White or Ecru.	*50 balls of White or Ecru.*

MILWARD'S STEEL CROCHET HOOK *No. 9.*

GAUGE:

Each motif measures 4 inches across center from point to point. For a single size spread 72 x 108 inches, make 18 x 27 motifs. For a double size spread 88 x 108 inches, make 22 x 27 motifs.

FIRST MOTIF . . . Starting at center, ch 8. Join with sl st. **1st rnd:** 16 s c in ring. Join to 1st s c. **2nd rnd:** S c in same place as sl st, (ch 5, skip 1 s c, s c in next s c) 7 times; ch 5, sl st in 1st s c (8 loops). **3rd rnd:** Sl st to center of next loop, ch 5, d c in same loop, * ch 3, in next loop make d c, ch 2 and d c. Repeat from * around, joining last ch-3 with sl st to 3rd st of 1st ch-5. **4th rnd:** Sl st in next loop, ch 3, in same loop make 2 d c, ch 2 and 3 d c; * s c in ch-3 loop, in next ch-2 loop make 3 d c, ch 2 and 3 d c. Repeat from * around, ending with s c in ch-3 loop, sl st in 3rd st of ch-3 first made. **5th rnd:** Sl st in each st and in 1st ch-2 sp, s c in same sp, * ch 8, s c in next ch-2 sp. Repeat from * around. Join. **6th rnd:** 12 s c in each loop (96 s c). Join with sl st. **7th rnd:** S c in each s c

around. Join. **8th rnd:** * Ch 9, skip 5 s c, s c in next s c. Repeat from * around. Join (16 loops). **9th rnd:** Sl st to center st of next loop, 5 s c in same loop, 5 s c in next loop, * ch 8, 5 s c in next 2 loops. Repeat from * around, ending with ch 8. Join to 1st s c. **10th rnd:** * Ch 10, 10 s c in ch-8 loop. Repeat from * around. Join. **11th rnd:** * Ch 5, in next loop make s c, ch 5 and s c; ch 5, skip 1 s c, s c in next 8 s c. Repeat from * around. Join. **12th rnd:** * 2 s c in next loop, ch 5, s c in next loop, ch 5, 2 s c in next loop, s c in each st across s c-group. Repeat from * around. Join. **13th rnd:** * S c in each st across s c-group, 2 s c in next loop, ch 7, 2 s c in next loop. Repeat from * around. Join and fasten off.

SECOND MOTIF . . . Like First Motif to 12th rnd incl. **13th rnd:** * S c in each st across s c-group, 2 s c in next loop, ch 3, sl st in any free ch-7 loop of First Motif, ch 3, 2 s c in next loop back on Second Motif. Continue as for 13th rnd of First Motif, joining the next point as previous point was joined and complete rnd. Fasten off.

Make necessary number of motifs, joining to adjacent motifs as Second was joined to First.

FILL-IN LACE . . . Starting at center, ch 6. Join. **1st rnd:** 16 s c in ring. Join. **2nd rnd:** S c in same place as sl st, (ch 7, skip 1 s c, s c in next s c) 7 times; ch 7, sl st in 1st s c (8 loops). **3rd rnd:** Sl st to center of 1st ch-7 loop, s c in same loop, * ch 8, sl st in joining between motifs, ch 8, s c back in same ch-7 loop, ch 4, s c in next ch-7 loop, ch 4, sl st in center of s c-group on motif, ch 4, s c back in same loop of Fill-In Motif, ch 4, s c in next ch-7 loop. Repeat from * around. Join. Fasten off.

Fill in all spaces between joinings in same way. Block to measurements given.

Dawn o' Day

Star-strewn, like early morn . . . a spread with a radiance about it. Made in the popular octagon medallion that women like to do so much. Let it take the spotlight in your bedroom.

Highly original and very lovely—this checkerboard of filet squares alternating with squares of Irish Crochet motifs—smart in modern or period settings.

American Way

MATERIALS: Use one of the following threads:

CLARK'S O.N.T. LUSTERSHEEN, *39 skeins of White or Ecru, or 52 skeins of any color for single size spread; 47 skeins of White or Ecru, or 62 skeins of any color for double size spread.*

J. & P. COATS KNIT-CRO-SHEEN, *52 balls of White or Ecru, or 63 balls of any color for single size spread; 62 balls of White or Ecru, or 74 balls of any color for double size spread.*

MILWARD'S *steel crochet hook No. 8.*

GAUGE: Each completed flower block or filet block measures 7 inches square. For a single size spread, about 77 x 105 inches, make 83 flower blocks, and 82 filet blocks. For a double size spread, about 91 x 105 inches, make 98 flower blocks and 97 filet blocks.

FLOWER BLOCK. First Motif... Ch 12, join. **1st rnd:** 16 s c in ring. Join. **2nd rnd:** Ch 5 (to count as s c and ch-4), * skip 1 s c, s c in next s c, ch 4. Repeat from * around, joining last ch-4 to 1st ch of ch-5. **3rd rnd:** Ch 4, sl st in s c following loop on previous row. Continue thus around, join. **4th rnd:** In each loop of 2nd rnd make s c, half d c, 3 d c, half d c and s c. Join to 1st s c made (8 petals). Sl st in 1st loop of 3rd rnd (at back of petal), sl st in 2nd ch of loop. **5th rnd:** S c in loop, * ch 5, s c in next loop. Repeat from * around, joining last loop to 1st s c made. Sl st to 3rd ch of 1st loop. **6th rnd:** Ch 5 (to count as d tr); make 2 d tr in ch at base of ch-5, holding back on hook the last loop of each st; thread over and draw through all loops, ch 1 tightly (a beginning cluster); make 3 more ch; make 3 d tr in same ch as

previous cluster, holding back last loop of each st; complete cluster. * Ch 3 more; in 3rd ch of next ch-5 make 2 clusters separated by ch-3. Repeat from *, joining last ch-3 to tip of 1st cluster made. Fasten off securely.

Second Motif... Work as for 1st motif to 5th rnd incl. **6th rnd:** Ch 5 and complete a beginning cluster, ch 1 more, drop loop from hook, insert it in a loop between 2-cluster group on 1st motif and draw loop through; ch 2, make a cluster in same ch as previous cluster, ch 3, cluster in 3rd ch of next ch-5, ch 1, drop loop from hook and join as before to corresponding loop of 1st motif, ch 2, cluster in same ch as previous cluster, ch 3. Complete as for 6th rnd of 1st motif (no more joinings).

Make a block consisting of 3 x 3 motifs (9 motifs in all), joining 2 cluster-groups at each corresponding side (see illustration).

Attach thread at ch-3 of 1st cluster-group on 1st motif at upper right. **1st rnd:** * 2 s c in ch-3 sp, s c at tip of cluster, 4 s c in ch-3 between groups, s c at tip of next cluster, 2 s c in next sp, ch 5, tr in center ch of next ch-3, ch 2, tr in 1st ch of ch-3 on next motif (this is ch following ch-1 belonging to cluster), ch 5. Repeat from * along this side, ending with 2 s c to correspond with beginning, ch 5; in center ch of ch-3 at corner make tr, ch 5, tr; ch 5. Repeat from beginning of rnd, joining last ch-5 to 1st s c made. **2nd rnd:** Ch 5 (to count as d c and ch-2), * skip 2 sts, d c in next st, ch 2. Repeat from * to 1st tr at corner; in center ch of corner ch-5 make d c, ch 5 and d c; ch 2, d c in next tr. Continue to make sps around; join last ch-2 to 3rd st of beginning ch-5 (27 sps along each side, counting corner sps). Fasten off securely.

FILET BLOCK... Starting at bottom, ch 86. **1st row:** D c in 8th ch from hook, * ch 2, skip 2 ch, d c in next ch. Repeat from * across (27 sps). Ch 5, turn. **2nd row:** D c in next d c, 2 d c in sp, d c in next d c (bl); make another bl, ch 2, d c in next d c; 2 more sps, 5 bls, 2 sps, 1 bl, 2 sps, 5 bls, 3 sps, 2 bls, 1 sp. Ch 5, turn. Now follow chart to top. Fasten off.

Make necessary number of blocks. Sew together neatly on wrong side, alternating blocks as in illustration, and having flower blocks at corners (for double size, 13 x 15 blocks; for single size, 11 x 15 blocks). Be sure rows of all filet blocks run in same direction.

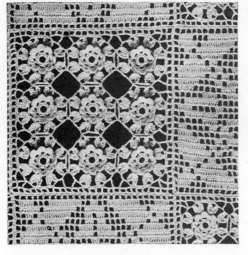

Stitch Detail of Motif

Chart for Filet Block

Nosegay

Lacy and lovely, these delightful old fashioned flower bouquet motifs are surrounded by delicate star-petal joinings . . . making a spread of dreamlike beauty. A design for future generations to cherish.

Nosegay

MATERIALS:

CLARK'S O.N.T. or J. & P. COATS BIG BALL BEST SIX CORD MERCERIZED CROCHET, *size 20*

SINGLE SIZE
44 balls of White or Ecru.

DOUBLE SIZE
58 balls of White or Ecru.

MILWARD'S STEEL CROCHET HOOK No. 8 or 9.

GAUGE:

Each motif measures 4 inches in diameter after blocking. For a single size spread about 68 x 104 inches, make 17 x 26 motifs. For a double size spread about 92 x 104 inches, make 23 x 26 motifs.

MOTIF . . . Starting at center, ch 8. Join with sl st. **1st rnd:** Ch 3 (to count as 1 d c), 19 d c in ring. Join with sl st to top st of ch-3 first made (20 sts). **2nd rnd:** Ch 3, d c in same place as sl st, 2 d c in each d c around. Join with sl st (40 sts). **3rd rnd:** * Ch 7, skip 3 d c, s c in next d c. Repeat from * around, ending with ch 3, skip 3 d c, tr in same place as sl st (10 loops). **4th rnd:** Ch 6, d c in top of tr, * ch 3, in center ch of next ch-7 loop make d c, ch 3 and d c. Repeat from * around, ending with ch 3, sl st in 3rd st of ch-6 first made. **5th rnd:** Ch 3, * 4 d c in next ch-3 sp, d c in next d c, ch 3, d c in next d c. Repeat from * around, ending with ch-3, sl st in 3rd st of ch-3 first made. **6th rnd:** Ch 3, d c in next 5 d c, * ch 3, s c in next sp, ch 3, d c in next 6 d c. Repeat from * around, ending with ch 3, sl st in 3rd st of ch-3 first made. **7th rnd:** * Ch 7, skip 4 d c, s c in next d c, ch 7, d c in next d c. Repeat from * around, ending with ch 3, tr in same place as sl st on previous rnd. **8th rnd:** Ch 3, 4 d c in top of tr, * ch 2, 5 d c in center st of next loop. Repeat from * around, ending rnd with half d c in 3rd st of ch-3 first made. **9th rnd:** S c in sp, ch 1, d c between ch-3 and following d c of next d c-group, * ch 1, d c between 2nd and 3rd d c of same group, ch 1, d c between 3rd and 4th d c, ch 1, d c between 4th and 5th d c of same group, ch 1, s c in next sp (between groups), ch 1, d c between 1st and 2nd d c of next d c-group. Repeat from * around, ending with ch 1, sl st in s c first made. **10th rnd:** S c in same place as sl st, * ch 5, skip 2 d c, in next sp make d c, ch 3 and d c; ch 5, skip 2 d c, s c in next s c. Repeat from * around, ending with ch 5, sl st in s c first made. Fasten off. This completes one motif.

SECOND MOTIF . . . Work as for First Motif to 9th rnd incl. **10th rnd:** S c in same place as sl st, ch 5, skip 2 d c, d c in next sp, ch 1, sl st in a point on First Motif, ch 1, d c back in same sp on Second Motif as last d c was made, ch 5, skip 2 d c, s c in next s c,

ch 5, skip 2 d c, d c in next sp, ch 1, sl st in next point on First Motif, ch 1, d c back in same sp on Second Motif as last d c was made, and continue in this manner until 3 points are joined. Complete rnd as for First Motif. Fasten off.

Make necessary number of motifs, joining as Second Motif was joined to First, leaving 2 points free between joinings.

FILL-IN LACE . . . Starting at center, ch 8. Join with sl st to form ring. Ch 5, 2 d tr in ring, holding back the last loop of each d tr on hook, thread over and draw through all loops on hook (a cluster), sl st in a free point (between joinings of motifs), * ch 6, s c in ring, ch 5, and complete another cluster in ring as before, sl st in next free point. Repeat from * around, ending with ch 6 after last cluster, sl st at base of ch-5 first made. Fasten off. Fill in all spaces in this manner.

Coquette

MATERIALS:

SINGLE SIZE
J. & P. COATS BEDSPREAD COTTON
14 balls of White or Ecru.

DOUBLE SIZE
J. & P. COATS BEDSPREAD COTTON
18 balls of White or Ecru.

MILWARD'S STEEL CROCHET HOOK *No. 7.*

GAUGE:

Each block measures about 7 inches square. For a single size spread about 72 x 106 inches, make 10 x 15 blocks. For a double size spread about 90 x 106 inches, make 13 x 15 blocks.

FIRST BLOCK . . . Starting at center, ch 10. Join with sl st to form ring. **1st rnd:** Ch 3, 23 d c in ring. Join with sl st to top of ch-3. **2nd rnd:** Ch 3, then holding back on hook the last loop of each d c, make 3 d c in same place as sl st, thread over and draw through all loops on hook (a d c-cluster made); * ch 5, then holding back on hook the last loop of each tr, make 4 tr in next st, thread over and draw through all loops on hook (a tr-cluster made), ch 5, then holding back on hook the last loop of each d c, make 4 d c in next st and complete cluster as before; ch 5, skip 3 d c, a 4-d c cluster in next d c. Repeat from * around, ending with ch 2, d c in tip of 1st cluster made. **3rd rnd:** Ch 5, d c in same place as last d c, * ch 2, d c in next sp, ch 2, in tip of next cluster make d c, ch 3 and d c, (ch 2, d c in next sp, ch 2, d c in tip of next cluster) twice. Repeat from * around, ending with ch 2, sl st

in 3rd st of ch 5. **4th rnd:** Ch 5, d c in next d c, (ch 2, d c in next d c) twice; ch 2, in next (corner) sp make d c, ch 3 and d c; ch 2, d c in next d c, and continue to make ch-2 sps around, working remaining corners as 1st corner was worked, and ending rnd as before. **5th and 6th rnds:** Ch 5 and make ch-2 sps around, working corners and joining rnds as before. **7th rnd:** Ch 3, * 2 d c in next sp, d c in d c, d c in next sp, d c in d c. Repeat from * around, making 5 d c in each corner sp. Join to top of ch-3.

8th rnd: Ch 8 (to count as tr and ch-4), skip 2 d c, s c in next d c, (ch 4, skip 2 d c, tr in next d c, ch 4, skip 2 d c, s c in next d c) twice; * ch 3, skip 1 d c, make a d c-cluster in next d c, ch 3, in next d c make a tr-cluster, ch 3 and a tr-cluster; ch 3, d c-cluster in next d c, ch 3, skip 1 d c, s c in next d c, (ch 4, skip 2 d c, tr in next d c, ch 4, skip 2 d c, s c in next d c) 5 times. Repeat from * around, ending with ch 4, sl st in 4th st of ch-8. **9th rnd:** Ch 8 (to count as d c and ch-5), (d c in next tr, ch 5) twice; * make a d c-cluster in sp between next 2 clusters, ch 3, in next sp make a tr-cluster, ch 5 and a tr-cluster; ch 3, make a d c-cluster in next sp, (ch 5, d c in next tr) 5 times; ch 5. Repeat from * around. Join to 3rd st of ch-8. **10th rnd:** Ch 8, s c in next sp, (ch 4, tr in next d c, ch 4, s c in next sp) twice; * ch 3, d c-cluster in next sp (between 2 clusters), ch 5, in next sp make a tr-cluster, ch 5 and a tr-cluster; ch 5, d c-cluster in next sp, ch 3, s c in next sp, (ch 4, tr in next d c, ch 4, s c in next sp) 5 times. Repeat from * around. Join to 4th st of ch-8. **11th rnd:** Ch 8, d c in next tr, ch 5, d c in next tr, * ch 6, make a d c-cluster in sp between next 2 clusters, ch 5, in next sp make a tr-cluster, ch 7 and a tr-cluster; ch 5, make a d c-cluster in next sp, ch 6, d c in next tr, (ch 5, d c in next tr) 4 times. Repeat from * around. Join to 3rd st of ch-8. **12th rnd:** Ch 3, (5 d c in next sp, d c in next st) 4 times; * in corner sp make 6 d c, ch 3 and 6 d c; d c in next st, (5 d c in next sp, d c in next st) 8 times. Repeat from * around. Join and fasten off.

Make necessary number of blocks and sew together on wrong side with neat over-and-over stitches.

Coquette

A superlative spread . . . dramatic in the very size of
its squares. Altogether charming in the crisp, fresh filagree work
framing the checked centers that hold a dainty flower encased.

Victoria Regina

MATERIALS: J. & P. COATS BIG BALL BEST SIX CORD MERCERIZED CROCHET, *size 30, 12 balls of Green for background and 6 balls of another color for flowers. If desired, use only White or Ecru, 13 balls.*

MILWARD'S *steel crochet hook No. 10 or 11.*

12¼ yds. of dotted Swiss, 36 inches wide; or 8½ yds. of organdie or muslin, 44 inches wide.

GAUGE: 6 sps make 1 inch; 6 rows make 1 inch.

INSERTION... Starting at bottom of chart, with Green ch 138 (18 ch sts to 1 inch). **1st row:** D c in 4th ch from hook, d c in next 2 ch; (ch 2, skip 2 ch, d c in next ch) 5 times—*5 sps made.* D c in next 9 ch—*3 bls made;* make 12 sps, 2 bls, 21 sps, 1 bl. Ch 3, turn. **2nd row:** Skip 1st d c, d c in next 3 d c—*bl over bl;* ch 2, d c in next d c—*sp over sp;* 11 more sps, ch 2; drop Green, attach 2nd color; holding Green at top of previous row and working over it to conceal it, make d c in next d c; (d c in next 2 ch, d c in next d c) 5 times, leaving the last 2 loops of last d c on hook. Drop 2nd color, pick up Green and draw through the 2 loops. Continuing with Green, make 2 sps, 3 bls, 10 sps, 5 bls, 5 sps, 1 bl. Ch 3, turn.

3rd row: With Green make 1 bl, 6 sps, 5 bls, 10 sps, 1 bl, ch 2. Drop Green, pick up 2nd color; holding Green at top of previous row to conceal it, make 1 sp, d c in next 2 ch, d c in next d c, d c in next 2 ch, d c in next d c, taking care to insert hook under the 2nd-color thread in order to conceal the carried strand. Continue to make d c over d c until 7 bls are made; make 2 more bls, leaving the last 2 loops of last d c on hook. Drop 2nd color, pick up Green and draw through the 2 loops on hook; make 11 Green sps, 1 bl. Ch 3, turn. **4th row:** 1 bl, 9 sps, ch 2; drop Green, pick up 2nd color and make d c in next d c. Holding Green at top of previous row and working over it, make 11 bls, leaving the last 2 loops of last d c on hook. Drop 2nd color, pick up Green and draw through remaining 2 loops; make 2 Green sps, ch 2. Drop Green, attach another ball of 2nd color and, working over Green, make d c in next d c, 5 bls, leaving the last 2 loops on hook. Drop 2nd color, pick up Green and draw through 2 loops on hook; make 4 Green sps, 4 bls, 6 sps, 1 bl. Ch 3, turn. Starting at 5th row, follow chart to top (rose design is worked in 2nd color), always concealing unused color as before and carrying it only so far as necessary (never carry unused color over sps). When rose design is completed, fasten off 2nd color securely and continue to follow chart, working with Green only. Then repeat entire design 6 more times. Piece should measure 83½ inches. Fasten off. Make another piece like this. Then make another piece 42 inches long, but start this piece at the 37th row on chart (instead of 1st row); then repeat entire design for required length, ending to correspond with beginning.

For top of spread, cut a piece of material 28 x 84½ inches. Make a ½-inch hem around all edges. With neat over-and-over stitches, sew a long strip of lace to each long edge. Sew short strip of lace to short edge (this is bottom of spread). Cut 2 strips of material, each 7 x 98 inches, and make a ½-inch hem along 1 short and 2 long edges. Placing unfinished side of strip at bottom, sew a strip neatly to each long edge of lace. Cut another strip 7 x 55 inches; hem both long edges and sew to bottom of spread, mitering corners to fit corners of lace. Cut 2 strips of material, 20 x 135 inches; make a 1-inch hem along 1 long edge and a ¼-inch hem along 2 short edges. Sew the unfinished long edge to long side of spread, easing in the extra fullness evenly to 97 inches. Finish other long side in the same way. Cut another piece of material, 20 x 82 inches; make a 1-inch hem along one long edge and a ¼-inch hem along 2 short edges. Sew the unfinished long edge to bottom of spread, easing in the extra fullness evenly to 54 inches.

Like the flower that turns its face toward the sun—this splendid motif has a nubby center from which contrasting petals radiate in a sunburst of beauty!

Sunflower

MATERIALS: Use one of the following threads:

CLARK'S O.N.T. LUSTERSHEEN—*Single Size: 21 skeins of White or Ecru and 12 skeins of any color for popcorn centers. Double Size: 27 skeins of White or Ecru and 15 skeins of any color for popcorn centers.*

J. & P. COATS KNIT-CRO-SHEEN—*Single Size: 28 balls of White or Ecru and 14 balls of any color for popcorn centers. Double Size: 36 balls of White or Ecru and 18 balls of any color for popcorn centers.*

MILWARD'S *steel crochet hook No. 6 or 7.*

GAUGE: Each block measures 9½ inches in diameter (excluding points). For a single size spread, about 72 x 108 inches, make 7 x 11 blocks. For a double size spread, about 92 x 108 inches, make 9 x 11 blocks.

FIRST BLOCK... Starting at center, with color ch 2. **1st rnd:** 9 s c in 2nd ch from hook. Join with sl st to 2nd ch of ch-2. **2nd rnd:** Ch 3 (to count as d c), 4 d c in same place as sl st, remove hook, insert it in 3rd st of ch-3 and draw dropped loop through —*pc st made.* (Ch 5, skip 1 s c, pc st of 5 d c in back loop of next s c) 4 times; ch 5, sl st in st directly be-

hind tip of 1st pc st. **3rd rnd:** Ch 3, pc st in same place as sl st, * ch 4, pc st in 3rd st of next ch-5, ch 4, pc st in st directly behind next pc st. Repeat from * around, ending with ch-4. Join. **4th rnd:** Ch 3, pc st in same place as sl st, * ch 2, pc st in 2nd st of ch-4, ch 2, pc st in st directly behind next pc st. Repeat from * around, ending with ch 2, sl st in st directly behind tip of 1st pc st (20 pc sts). **5th rnd:** Make pc st directly behind each pc st, with ch-3 between pc sts. Join. **6th rnd:** Same as 4th rnd, making pc sts in 2nd ch of ch-3 (40 pc sts). **7th rnd:** Same as 5th rnd. Fasten off. **8th rnd:** Attach White (or Ecru) in st directly behind 1st pc st, ch 3, 2 d c in ch-3, d c in st behind next pc st, 3 d c in next ch-3 sp. * Ch 1, skip next pc st, 3 d c in next ch-3 sp, d c in st behind next pc st, 3 d c in next sp. Repeat from * around, ch 1, join (20 dc-groups). **9th rnd:** Ch 3, d c in 6 d c, * ch 2, d c in next 7 d c. Repeat from * around, ch 2. Join. **10th and 11th rnds:** Same as 9th rnd, making ch-3 between d c-groups on 10th rnd and ch-4 between d c-groups on 11th rnd. **12th rnd:** Ch 3, d c in next 2 d c; * d c in next 2 d c, holding back the last loop of each d c on hook; thread over and draw through all loops on hook (d c decreased); d c in next 2 d c, ch 6, d c in next 3 d c. Repeat from * around, ch 6, join. **13th rnd:** Ch 3, d c in next d c, * work off next 2 d c as 1 d c, d c in next 2 d c, ch 2, skip 1 ch, d c in next 4 ch, ch 2, d c in next 2 d c. Repeat from * around. Ch 2, join. **14th rnd:** Ch 3, d c in next d c. * Dec. 1 d c as before, d c in next d c, ch 3, d c in next 4 d c, ch 3, d c in next 2 d c. Repeat from * around. Ch 3, join. **15th rnd:** Ch 3, * dec. 1 d c, d c in next d c, ch 5, d c in next d c. Repeat from * around. Ch 5, join. **16th rnd:** Ch 3, * dec. 1 d c, ch 6, d c in next d c. Repeat from * around. Ch 6, join. **17th rnd:** Ch 3, d c in next d c, ch 7, * d c in next 2 d c, working them off as 1 d c; ch 7. Repeat from * around, join. **18th rnd:** Sl st in next d c, ch 11, * d c in next d c, ch 8. Repeat from * around, join. **19th rnd:** Ch 1, * s c in next 8 ch, s c in next d c, s c in next 8 ch, ch 20, s c in 2nd ch from hook and in each ch across (center vein of leaf), s c in next d c, s c in next 8 ch, s c in next d c. Ch 4, turn. (Skip 2 s c of center vein, d tr in next s c, ch 3) 4 times; skip 2 s c, tr in next s c, ch 4, skip 4 s c, s c in tip of vein, ch 4, skip 4 s c, tr in next s c; (ch 3, skip 2 s c, d tr in next s c) 4 times. Ch 4, sl st in 9th s c, counting from center vein; sl st in next s c, turn. S c in next 4 ch, ch 5, sl st in 5th ch from hook (p); s c in d tr; (s c in next 3 ch, p, s c in d tr) 3 times; s c in next 3 ch, p, s c in tr,

(Continued on page 44)

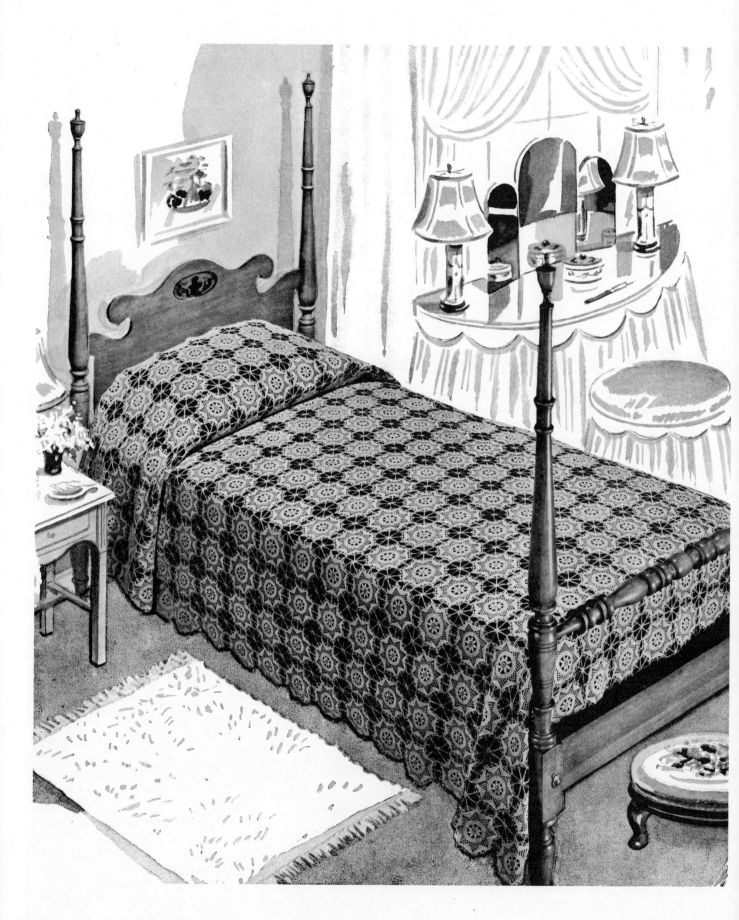

A significant new crochet pattern—spreading from its starlike center to a radiant pool—it deserves applause for its originality and distinction.

Ballerina

MATERIALS: Use one of the following threads in size 20, White or Ecru:

CLARK'S O.N.T. or J. & P. COATS BIG BALL BEST SIX CORD MERCERIZED CROCHET, *51 balls for single size spread; 61 balls for double size spread.*

CLARK'S BIG BALL MERCERIZED CROCHET, *36 balls for single size spread; 43 balls for double size spread.*

MILWARD'S *steel crochet hook No. 10.*

If a Heavier Thread Is Desired, See Instructions Following Fill-in Lace

GAUGE: Each motif measures 5 inches in diameter. For a single size spread, about 75 x 105 inches, make 15 x 21 motifs. For a double size spread, about 90 x 105 inches, make 18 x 21 motifs.

MOTIF... Starting at center, ch 8, join with sl st. **1st rnd:** Ch 5, * d c in ring, ch 2. Repeat from * 6 more times. Join to 3rd st of ch-5 (8 sps). **2nd rnd:** Sl st in next sp, ch 5, 4 d tr in same sp, holding back the last loop of each d tr on hook; thread over and

draw through all loops on hook (a cluster); * ch 8, 5 d tr in next sp, holding back the last loop of each d tr on hook; thread over and draw through all loops on hook (cluster). Repeat from * around, ending with ch 8, sl st at tip of 1st cluster made. **3rd rnd:** 10 s c in each sp (80 s c in rnd). **4th to 7th rnds incl:** S c in each s c, ending 7th rnd with sl st in next st. **8th rnd:** * Ch 5, skip 1 st, s c in next st, ch 5, skip 2 sts, s c in next st. Repeat from * around (32 loops). **9th rnd:** Sl st to center of next loop, 2 s c in loop, * ch 5, s c in next loop. Repeat from * 2 more times, ch 5, 2 s c in next loop, and continue thus around, ending with sl st in 1st s c made. **10th rnd:** Ch 1, s c in next 2 s c, * 2 s c in next loop; (ch 5, s c in next loop) twice, ch 5, 2 s c in next loop, s c in next 2 s c. Repeat from * around, ending with 2 s c in last loop, sl st in ch-1 first made. **11th rnd:** Ch 1, s c in next 4 s c, * 2 s c in next loop, ch 5, s c in next loop, ch 5, 2 s c in next loop, s c in next 6 s c. Repeat from * around, ending with sl st in ch-1 first made. **12th rnd:** Ch 1, s c in next 6 s c, * 2 s c in next loop, ch 7, 2 s c in next loop, s c in next 10 s c. Repeat from * around, ending rnd as before. **13th rnd:** Ch 1, s c in next 8 s c, * in ch-7 loop make 2 s c, ch 5, 2 s c; s c in next 14 s c. Repeat from * around; join. **14th rnd:** Ch 1, s c in each s c, making 5 s c in each ch-5 loop; join. **15th rnd:** Ch 1, s c in each s c, making 2 s c in center st of 5-s c group; join. **16th rnd:** S c in next s c, ch 6 (to count as d c and ch-3), d c in same place as last s c, * ch 6, skip 5 s c, s c in next s c, ch 6; in center s c at tip of next point make d c, ch 3, d c; ch 6, skip 5 s c, s c in next s c, ch 6, skip 5 s c; in next s c make d c, ch 3, d c. Repeat from * around, joining last ch-6 to 3rd st of ch-6 first made. **17th rnd:** Sl st in next ch, s c in sp, ch 6, d c in same sp, * ch 6, s c in next s c, ch 7; in sp at point make d c, ch 3, d c; ch 7, s c in next s c, ch 6; in next sp make d c, ch 3, d c. Repeat from * around. Join and fasten off.

Make necessary number of motifs. With over-and-over stitches sew 3 points of one motif (see illustration) to corresponding 3 points of adjacent motifs, thus leaving 1 point free on each motif between joinings.

FILL-IN LACE... Ch 10, join to form ring. * Ch 11, sl st in a free point between joinings; ch 11, s c back in ring. Ch 16,

(Continued on page 44)

Ballerina

(Continued)

sl st in joining; ch 16, s c in ring. Repeat from *
3 more times. Join and fasten off. Fill in all spaces
between joinings in same manner.

For a Bedspread of Heavier Thread:

MATERIALS: Use one of the following threads:
Clark's O. N. T. Lustersheen, *30 skeins of
White or Ecru, or 40 skeins of any color for
single size spread; 37 skeins of White or Ecru,
or 49 skeins of any color for double size spread.*

J. & P. Coats Knit-Cro-Sheen, *40 balls of
White or Ecru or 48 balls of any color for single
size spread; 49 balls of White or Ecru or 59 balls
of any color for double size spread.*

Milward's *steel crochet hook No. 6 or 7.*

Gauge: Each motif measures 6 inches in diameter.
For a single size spread, about 72 x 108 inches, make
12 x 18 motifs. For a double size spread, about
90 x 108 inches, make 15 x 18 motifs.

SUNFLOWER

(Continued from page 40)

s c in next 4 ch, p, s c in next s c, s c in next 4 ch, p,
s c in tr. (S c in next 3 ch, p, s c in d tr) 4 times; s c
in next 4 ch, s c in next d c; (s c in next 8 ch, p, s c
in d c) 7 times. Repeat from * around. Fasten off.

SECOND BLOCK... Work exactly as for first
block to within p at tip of 3rd leaf, ch 3, remove hook,
insert it in 3rd st of p at tip of leaf on 1st block and
draw loop through, ch 2, s c in 1st ch of ch-3; s c in
s c at tip of leaf back on 2nd block; s c in next 4 ch,
s c in tr, remove hook, insert it in next p back on 1st
block and draw loop through; s c in next 3 ch back on
2nd block, s c in d tr, ch 3, join to next p back on
1st block as 1st p was joined. S c in s c back on 2nd
block and complete leaf as before, s c in next 8 ch,
p, s c in next 8 ch. Join next p to corresponding p of
1st block as 1st p of leaf was joined; join next 3 p's
as 2nd p of leaf was joined; join following p as 1st p
was joined. Continue around 2nd block as for 1st
block, joining the 4th, 5th and 6th p's of next leaf to
corresponding p's of 1st block as p's were joined on
previous leaf. Complete as for 1st block. Fasten off.

THIRD BLOCK... Work exactly as for 2nd
block, joining the 3 p's of 3rd leaf to corresponding
p's of 1st block as before, and joining top p of next
leaf to same p on 1st block where top p of leaf on 2nd
block was joined.

FOURTH BLOCK... Join 2nd leaf of block
to corresponding leaf at lower edge of 3rd block, and
continue across 4th block, joining the center 5 p's (between leaves) as before and joining the top 5 p's of
next leaf to 3rd and 1st blocks and joining the center
p in same place as other blocks were joined. Continue
in this manner, joining other side in same way.

Make the necessary number of blocks, joining as
before.

Kimberley

MATERIALS:

J. & P. COATS KNIT-CRO-SHEEN

SINGLE SIZE
35 balls of White or Ecru,
or 52 balls of any color.

DOUBLE SIZE
48 balls of White or Ecru,
or 71 balls of any color.

Steel crochet hook No. 7 or 8.

GAUGE: 4 sps make 1 inch; 4 rows make 1 inch. Single size spread measures about 69 x 103 inches, including fringe. Double size spread measures about 91 x 108 inches, including fringe.

(Directions on page 47)

Sutton Place

MATERIALS:

CLARK'S O.N.T. MERCERIZED BEDSPREAD COTTON

SINGLE SIZE
36 balls of White or Ecru.

DOUBLE SIZE
48 balls of White or Ecru.

OR

J. & P. COATS KNIT-CRO-SHEEN

SINGLE SIZE
36 balls of White or Ecru,
or 58 balls of any color.

DOUBLE SIZE
48 balls of White or Ecru,
or 77 balls of any color.

Steel crochet hook No. 8.

GAUGE: 4 sps make 1 inch; 4 rnds make 1 inch. Completed block measures 7½ inches square. For a single size spread about 72 x 108 inches including fringe, make 9 x 14 blocks. For a double size spread about 90 x 108 inches including fringe, make 12 x 14 blocks.

Sutton Place

BLOCK . . . Starting at center, ch 9. **1st rnd:** In 9th ch from hook make (dc, ch 5) 3 times. Join with sl st in 4th st of 1st ch made. **2nd rnd:** Ch 3, in next sp make 3 dc, ch 5 and 3 dc; * dc in next dc, in next sp make 3 dc, ch 5 and 3 dc. Repeat from * around. Join with sl st in top st of 1st ch-3. **3rd rnd:** Ch 3, dc in next 3 dc, * in next sp make 3 dc, ch 5 and 3 dc; dc in 7 dc. Repeat from * around. Join. **4th rnd:** Ch 3, dc in 3 dc, * ch 2, skip 2 dc, dc in next dc, in next sp make 3 dc, ch 5 and 3 dc; dc in next dc, ch 2, skip 2 dc, dc in 7 dc. Repeat from * around. Join. **5th rnd:** Ch 5, skip 2 dc, dc in next dc, * ch 2, dc in 4 dc, in corner sp make 3 dc, ch 5 and 3 dc; dc in 4 dc, ch 2, dc in next dc, (ch 2, skip 2 dc, dc in next dc) twice. Repeat from * around. Join with sl st in 3rd st of 1st ch

There are 10 spaces between heavy lines

made. Ch 5 for beginning of 6th rnd and follow chart for remainder of block, making ch 5 at corners. The 1st sp of 6th rnd is indicated by "X" on chart. Beginning of rnds is indicated on chart by heavy line.

Make necessary number of blocks and sew together on wrong side with neat over-and-over stitches.

TASSELS . . . Use a piece of cardboard 4 inches wide; place 2 strands each 5 inches long across length of cardboard. Wind 1 strand of thread 65 times around width of cardboard. Break off. Pick up the 5-inch lengths and tie securely. Slip tassel off cardboard, cut strands at untied end. Wind thread around tassel near top and tie. Trim evenly. Sew a tassel to edge of spread at each joining of blocks and at each corner on 1 narrow and 2 long edges.

FRINGE . . . Cut twelve 10-inch strands of thread. Double the strands forming a loop. Insert hook in sp following a corner sp on edge and pull loop through; then pull loose ends through loop and pull tight. Make 8 fringes evenly in sps on edge of each block. Block to measurements given.

Kimberley

(Illustrated on page 45)

Sizes	Single	Double

Make a chain 3 yards long (about 10 ch sts to 1 inch). **1st row:** Dc in 8th ch from hook, * ch 2, skip 2 ch, dc in next ch. Repeat from * until there are on row **245 sps 335 sps** Cut off remaining ch. Ch 5, turn.

2nd row: Dc in next dc (sp over sp), * ch 2, dc in next dc. Repeat from * across, ending with ch 2, dc in 5th st of turning ch. There are **245 sps 335 sps** Ch 5, turn.

3rd row: (This is right side.) Dc in next dc (sp over sp), make 16 more sps, * make a pc st in next sp—*to make a pc st, ch 1, 5 dc in sp, drop loop from hook, insert hook in ch-1 and draw dropped loop through*—dc in next dc, make 29 sps. Repeat from * across, ending with pc st, 17 sps. Ch 5, turn. **4th row:** Make 16 sps, * make a reverse pc st in next sp—*to make a reverse pc st, work as for pc st, only inserting hook in ch-1 from back of work, thus raising pc st to right side*—dc in next dc, ch 2, skip pc st, dc in next dc (sp over pc st), reverse pc st, 27 sps. Repeat from * across, ending with reverse pc st, sp, reverse pc st, 16 sps. Ch 5, turn. **5th row:** 15 sps, * (pc st, sp) twice; pc st, 25 sps. Repeat from * across, ending with (pc st, sp) twice; pc st, 15 sps. Ch 5, turn. **6th row:** 14 sps, * (reverse pc st, sp) 3 times; reverse pc st, 23 sps. Repeat from * across, ending with (reverse pc st, sp) 3 times; reverse pc st, 14 sps. Ch 5, turn. **7th row:** 13 sps, * (pc st, sp) 4 times; pc st, 21 sps. Repeat from * across, ending with (pc st, sp) 4 times; pc st, 13 sps. Ch 5, turn.

Starting with the 8th row follow chart to top. The repeat of pattern on each row is area between X's *(including sps marked with X's)*. Work end of each row to correspond with beginning. Continue thus repeating pattern (from 8th row to top of chart) until 10 large and 10 small diamonds have been made. Now work 8th to 30th rows incl and complete 11th large diamond and top of spread to correspond with beginning of piece. Fasten off.

FRINGE . . . Cut eight 10-inch strands. Double the strands, forming a loop. Insert hook in corner sp and draw loop through; then bring loose ends through loop and pull tight. Make a fringe in every other sp all around. Trim fringe evenly to measure 4 inches.

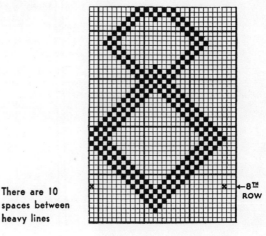

There are 10 spaces between heavy lines

←8TH ROW

Crochet Stitches

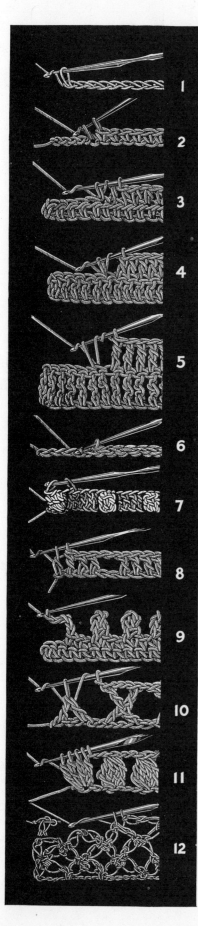

1...Chain (ch): Make loop in thread, insert hook in loop, and draw main length of thread through. Continue to draw thread through each new loop formed for length desired.

2...Single Crochet (s c): Insert hook under 2 loops of st, draw thread through st (2 loops on hook), thread over hook, draw through the 2 loops.

3...Half Double Crochet (half d c): Make like d c until there are 3 loops on hook; then thread over and draw through all 3 loops.

4...Double Crochet (d c): Thread over hook, insert hook in st, and draw thread through (3 loops on hook), thread over hook, draw through 2 loops, thread over, draw through 2 remaining loops.

5...Treble (tr): Thread over hook twice, insert hook in st and draw thread through st (4 loops on hook), thread over, draw through 2 loops, thread over, draw through 2 loops, thread over, draw through remaining 2 loops. For a **Double Treble (d tr)**, thread over hook 3 times; and for a **Triple Treble (tr tr)**, thread over hook 4 times, taking off 2 loops at a time as in the tr.

6...Slip Stitch (sl st): Insert hook through st, catch thread, and, with one motion, draw through both the st and the 1 loop on hook. The sl st is used for joining, or when an invisible st is required.

7...Popcorn Stitch (pc st): Ch 1, 5 d c in next st, drop st from hook, insert hook back in ch-1 and draw loop through the one on hook.

8...Block (bl) and Space (sp): Make 4 d c over 4 sts of preceding row (this forms 1 bl), ch 2, skip 2 sts, make 1 sp. The bl and sp are used in Filet Crochet.

9...Picot (p): Make a ch of 3, 4, or 5 sts, according to length of p desired, and s c in the foundation, or in 1st st of ch.

10...Cross Stitch: Thread over twice, insert hook in st and draw thread through as for a tr (4 loops on hook), thread over, and draw through 2 loops, thread over, skip 2 sts, insert hook in next st, draw thread through (5 loops on hook), thread over and draw off 2 loops at a time 4 times, ch 2, 1 d c in the center point of the cross, thus completing the cross.

11...Cluster: Make 3 or more tr in the same st, always holding the last loop of each tr on the hook; then, thread over hook and take off all remaining loops. Then make a tight ch to fasten the cluster.

12...Knot Stitch: Draw a loop on hook out ¼ inch, draw thread through, making a ch st of it. Put hook between loop and single thread of this ch and make an s c. Work another similar knot st, skip 4 sts of preceding row, 1 s c in next. Repeat from beginning to end of row. Make two ⅜-inch knot sts to turn, 1 s c over double loop at right of 1st center knot of preceding row, 1 s c over double loop at left of same knot, 2 knot sts and repeat.

ABBREVIATIONS for CROCHET

Chain	ch	Slip Stitch	sl st	Inclusive	incl.
Single Crochet	s c	Popcorn Stitch	pc st	Increase	inc.
Half Double Crochet	half d c	Block	bl	Decrease	dec.
Double Crochet	d c	Space	sp	Together	tog.
Treble	tr	Picot	p		
Double Treble	d tr	Stitch	st		
Triple Treble	tr tr	Round	rnd		

* (asterisk) When this symbol appears, continue working until instructions refer you back to this symbol.

THE END